Hope - Anchor of the Soul

Michael Gifford

Scriptures taken from the NEW KING JAMES VERSION®.
Copyright© 1982 by Thomas Nelson, Inc. Used by permission.
All rights reserved.

P.O. Box 3687
Cleburne, TX 76033
HopkinsPublishing.com

Copyright © 2015
ISBN-10: 1-62080-052-7
ISBN-13: 978-1-62080-052-2
Catalog record information is on file with the Library of Congress
Version 1.0

eBook:
ISBN-10: 1-62080-054-3
ISBN-13: 978-1-62080-054-6
LCCN: 2015948585

All rights reserved. This book or parts thereof may not be reproduced in any form without written permission from the publisher.

Discover Other Titles
By Hopkins Publishing
HopkinsPublishing.com

This book is dedicated to my Godly and beautiful wife, Emily, who is truly a blessing of hope in my life.

Table of Contents

Introduction vii

Chapter One: Hope - Anchor of the Soul 1

Chapter Two: Hope's Firm Foundation 11

Chapter Three: Hope's Partners in the Heart 23

Chapter Four: "Abandon Hope, All Ye Who Enter Here" . . . 35

Chapter Five: In Defense of Hope 47

Chapter Six: Hope and Obedience 59

Chapter Seven: Hope for Today 71

Chapter Eight: Hope in the Psalms 83

Chapter Nine: Hope in Jeremiah 95

Chapter Ten: Hope in Romans 107

Chapter Eleven: Inspiring Hope In Others 119

Chapter Twelve: Jesus' Victory – The Reason for Our Hope . . 131

Chapter Thirteen: Hope's Ultimate Fulfillment 143

Appendix: God's Plan of Salvation 155

Introduction

The word "hope" is used in a variety of ways in our world. A child hopes for a particular item for his or her birthday. A man gets his hopes up when an opportunity for a better job arises. A lady hopes that her boyfriend will propose to her. A traveler passing through a storm hopes that the bad weather will pass. Each of these hopes represents an expectation, an anticipation of something good. Hope is a positive thought or feeling. Its value and desirability are summed up in the well worn phrase, "There's always hope."

As happy and peaceful as hope can be in the scenarios of the previous paragraph, it takes on a much greater meaning when it comes from the mouth of God and the pens of His inspired writers in the Bible. The Lord said in Isaiah 55:8-9, "For My thoughts *are* not your thoughts, Nor *are* your ways My ways," says the LORD. "For *as* the heavens are higher than the earth, So are My ways higher than your ways, And My thoughts than your thoughts." As together we study the precious word "hope" in this book, let us allow the Lord's usage of it to lead us into even deeper joy and peace.

The hope offered by God is not a mere wish like the child's hope for a present. It is not an ordinary earthly desire like the man's hope for a better job. It is not controlled by the feelings of a man like the lady's hope is controlled by her boyfriend's desire or lack of desire to marry her. It is not temporary like the hope of the traveler. No, the hope of which we read in the Bible is long-lasting and can, in fact, be life-lasting because it is the hope that God provides. Hope that finds its basis and fulfillment in the Lord is, therefore, far above anything this world can produce. It is a genuine guardian of the heart to protect us against despair throughout our earthly days.

May this book cause its readers to search the Scriptures more diligently and find that hope that God offers and that we all want. "Blessed *is* the man who trusts in the Lord, And whose hope is the Lord." (Jeremiah 17:7).

Michael Gifford
August 2015

Chapter One

Hope – Anchor of the Soul

Memory Work:

"This *hope* we have as an anchor of the soul, both sure and steadfast, and which enters the *Presence* behind the veil." (Hebrews 6:19)

What comes to mind when you think of an anchor? Do you think of something heavy and sturdy? Do you picture a huge ship being held in place in storm-stirred waters? Does your mind turn to thoughts of something that is stable and firmly grounded? If you pondered any of these images then you have a good grasp of an anchor's purpose and usefulness. Anchors are designed to prevent their watercraft from drifting. They do so, not only by virtue of their weight and sturdiness, but also by virtue of their hooking onto a solid bed beneath the water's surface.

The title of this book and of this chapter and the verse from which both come are found in a Divinely inspired New Testament epistle written to Christians who were drifting spiritually. For some of them, the pressures of the world had become overwhelming. Their hands were hanging down and their knees were buckling (Hebrews 12:12). Their strength was waning, if not already gone, and they were gradually heading back into the dangerous sea of sin.

In the sentences leading up to Hebrews 6:19, the inspired writer reminded his readers of the great promises of God. Because of God's promises and His faithfulness to His promises, they could have tremendous comfort ("strong consolation"). He then reminded them that they had fled for refuge and laid hold of hope. The English phrase, "fled for refuge" is actually the translation of a single Greek word. It indicates one's flight to a safe haven. While various commentators suggest that the remote reference here is to the Old Testament cities of refuge (Numbers 35:6ff), it's clear that the immediate reference is to the original readers' turning to God for salvation in their obedience to the Gospel. They found safety in the blood of Christ when they became Christians (Acts 4:12). Not only that, they found hope, the hope that would anchor them in their struggles against the pull of the world.

It's interesting, but not at all coincidental, that these words are essentially part of a parentheses that begins in Hebrews 5:11. The inspired writer had wanted to talk to these brethren about Melchizedek. He had many things that he wanted to say about the king of Salem, each of which would have been beneficial to the readers in their defense of the faith. He wasn't able to go into as much detail as he would have liked to though because they had stopped growing and could not handle the depth of knowledge that he wished to impart to them. In Hebrews 5:11-6:8 we find a rebuke for their spiritual indolence. Hebrews 6:9 launches a series of encouraging words, beginning with, "But, beloved, we are confident of better things concerning you." He knew they could do better. He was confident that they could grow beyond the first principles of the faith. He was certain that they could build the spiritual muscle needed to fend off the attacks they were facing. Thus, he encouraged them to remember the faith and patience of those who had gone before (Hebrews 6:12). God had made promises to their forefathers in faith and had kept each and every one of them. God had made promises to these children of His as well. He would keep the promises. He would bless here on earth and, ultimately, in eternity. What these early Christians needed to do was to go back and recall the refuge they found in God when they obeyed the Gospel and then hold onto the hope that they realized at that time. This hope would ground them, sustain them and move them along to greater spiritual heights.

In an effort to make personal application of these Bible passages, let us each take stock of our own spiritual lives. If we are living in a Godly manner, we are daily confronting the pull of the world just like these first century Christians were. Paul wrote, "Yes, and all who desire to live godly in Christ Jesus will suffer persecution." (II Timothy 3:12). There is a depth of faith which we can attain and which will, in turn, feed our hope in the face of adversity. But are we distracted? We did not let anything distract us when we initially ran to God for refuge in obeying His Gospel. Do you remember the joy and peace and hope you felt when you had your sins washed away by the blood of Christ (Acts 8:36-39)? Do you still have all of that? Is your hope greater or smaller than the moment that you arose from the water as a new creature (II Corinthians 5:17)? Are you distracted from growing in the faith and feeding your hope? Of course, God is not going to speak audibly to any of us today, but if He did, would He have to talk to you and me like He did to the original readers of the letter to the Hebrews? Would He have to interrupt His words of encouragement to us and rebuke us for not putting forth the effort to be stronger in the faith? It's clear to see from the inspired text that hope is a great blessing that can carry us through the darkest night. It's also clear to see that hope is developed and strengthened when we purposefully and diligently seek the source of that hope, God Himself.

Verse 19 defines the focus of hope. It serves as an anchor, but, more specifically, it is an anchor of the soul. God wants all souls to be saved (I Timothy 2:4; II Peter 3:9). He takes no pleasure in the loss of souls (Ezekiel 33:11). Were He not the loving God that He is, He would have given up on His human creation upon the first act of disobedience. Instead, Romans 5:8 states, "But God demonstrates His own love toward us, in that while we were still sinners, Christ died for us."

In contrast to God's desire to save souls is Satan's determination to condemn souls. Jesus called Him the father of lies (John 8:44). He is the source of the tempestuous waves that threaten to loosen the Divine anchor that moors our souls. He doesn't just want to injure us. He wants to devour us (I Peter 5:8).

God is focused on our souls. Satan is as well. God has given us hope as an anchor for our souls. Satan utilizes such tools as fear, worry, and mistrust in his effort to tear the anchor away. With these opposing forces in mind, let's go back to the words, "lay hold" in verse 18. They are translated from a single Greek word. Other versions render this word, "take hold," "hold to," "hold fast," and "lay hold." In between God's source for anchoring our souls and Satan's tactics to separate our souls from the Lord is our personal effort to grab hold and not let go of that which God has given to us. Hope is indeed an anchor of the soul, but it must be developed and utilized. A literal anchor is of no value to its vessel if it lies unused on the deck. Hope will not anchor our souls if it is not held in the heart and developed through God's Word.

Not only does verse 19 define the focus of hope, it also describes the qualities of hope. The hope that a Christian has in God is "both sure and steadfast." "Both" indicates that these two qualities are on equal footing. All four words combined form a superlative. The anchor of hope that God provides is the strongest, most reliable, most certain hope that can be found anywhere.

As suggested in this book's introduction, the hope found in God is more than a wish. It transcends a mere desire. This hope is sure and steadfast because of its firm foundation. More will be said about hope's firm foundation in the next chapter but, for now, consider this statement made by Paul as recorded in Colossians 1:5 as evidence of how sure and steadfast God's hope is: "because of the hope which is laid up for you in heaven, of which you heard before in the word of the truth of the gospel." Paul's letter to the Colossian Christians was written to encourage them to abide in Christ. They were being tempted to go beyond the doctrine of Christ by both Gnostic and Jewish influences. The apostle's introductory comments commended them for the faith they had demonstrated, the love they had shown to the saints and the hope to which they had held. The hope that was in their hearts was heavenly in its origin as well as its realization. They had developed it through the Word of God. Their hope that allowed them to stay strong was firmly grounded in eternity with God. Nothing in this world can surpass this hope for its foundation is Divine. It is, indeed, "both sure and steadfast."

Verse 19 defines the focus of hope, describes the qualities of hope, and also designates the fruition of hope. It enters into the veil. "The veil" is a reference to the curtain that separated the Holy of Holies from the rest of the Jewish temple (Hebrews 9:3). In Hebrews 6:19, however, the literal veil of the earthly temple is not under consideration. Instead, the veil is used here as an image. Beginning in Hebrews 9:1, we find the writer expounding upon his reference to the literal veil. It was a shadow of something to come. It was a figure or type of something greater on the horizon. Hebrews 10:20 defines that which the literal veil foreshadowed as the flesh of Christ. His flesh was torn and His blood was shed so that mankind might enter heaven. Hebrews 9:24 says, "For Christ has not entered the holy places made with hands, *which are* copies of the true, but into heaven itself, now to appear in the presence of God for us." Jesus' death tore open the veil that separated mankind from the Holiest of Holies, heaven itself, and provided entrance for us through obedience to His Gospel. Going back to Hebrews 6, we see this truth affirmed in verse 20. Jesus has opened the veil, having gone into heaven itself as the forerunner. We can follow Him there (John 13:36-14:4). Hope leads us there. In fact, hope takes us right up to that point and enters with us into eternal life.

The anchor of hope holds us fast against Satan's attacks. When the angry waves of trial beat against us, hope keeps us looking up toward heaven instead of around at our troubles. It is a blessing that is to be grasped and held onto relentlessly. It is something that is to be continually developed and demonstrated in our lives. As we allow hope to keep us still and firmly grounded in the wake of the rising tides of evil, we will find that one day it will lead us to heaven's portals and, at last, take us home.

EXERCISE YOUR MIND

True or False

1. The original readers of the letter to the Hebrews were discouraged. T F
2. The original readers laid hold on hope when they obeyed the Gospel. T F
3. Satan tries to take our hope away from us. T F
4. It does not take any effort on our part to make hope stronger. T F
5. The veil in Hebrews 6:19 refers to the literal veil in the earthly temple. T F

Multiple Choice

1. Because of God's promises and His faithfulness to His promises:
   A) Christians should have doubts about His care for us;
   B) Christians can have tremendous comfort ("strong consolation");
   C) Christians can only cross their fingers and wish that God will care for them.

2. The inspired writer was not able to say all he wanted to about Melchisedec because:
   A) the readers had stopped growing spiritually;
   B) he did not have the time;
   C) it wasn't important.

3. The inspired writer knew that the readers:
   A) had no hope of ever growing spiritually;
   B) could do better;
   C) did not care about what he had to say.

4. God wants:
   A) all souls to be saved;
   B) only those predestined for heaven to be saved;
   C) no one to be saved.

5. Satan:
   A) is honest and helpful;
   B) wants us to be saved;
   C) is the father of lies.

Fill in the Blanks

(Note: All scripture quotations are taken from the New King James Version and can be found in this lesson.)

1. "But, _____, we are _____ of _____ things concerning _____."
2. "Yes, and all who _____ to live _____ in Christ Jesus will suffer _____."
3. "But God _____ His own _____ toward us, in that while we were still _____, Christ _____ for us."
4. "Because of the _____ which is laid up for you in _____, of which you _____ before in the _____ of the _____ of the _____."
5. "For _____ has not entered the _____ places made with _____, *which are* _____ of the _____, but into _____ itself, now to appear in the _____ of _____ for us."

Questions for Discussion

1. What other features of an anchor come to mind and how would these features help us spiritually? _____

2. What is the meaning of the phrase, "the hands which hang down, and the feeble knees" in Hebrews 12:12? _____

3. What are some ways in which we can strengthen discouraged Christians? _____

4. In what ways can we strengthen ourselves when we are discouraged? _____

5. What is a refuge? In what ways is God our refuge? _____

6. How does one lay hold of hope? _____

7. Why must Christians grow in knowledge of God's Word? _____

8. What are the dangers of not growing in knowledge of God's Word?

9. What do we need to do to make sure we are growing in knowledge of God's Word? _____

10. What are some things that we allow to distract us from growing spiritually? _____

11. How valuable is your soul? _____

12. What are some of the ways in which Satan attacks us? _____

13. After Jesus died, the veil of the temple was torn in two from top to bottom (Matthew 27:51). Is there any significance in that happening, and if so, what is it? _____

_____

_____

_____

14. What is the meaning of the word, "forerunner" as it applies to Jesus?

_____

_____

_____

15. Why was it important for Jesus to be the forerunner? _____

_____

_____

_____

SEARCH THE SCRIPTURES

(Note: For this section, you will find a good concordance helpful. All scripture quotations are taken from the New King James Version.)

Where is the following Bible verse located? _____

"For You are my hope, O Lord GOD; *You are* my trust from my youth."

Chapter Two

Hope's Firm Foundation

Memory Work:

"In hope of eternal life which God, who cannot lie, promised before time began." (Titus 1:2)

A promise is a very precious item. The word "promise" brings to mind a commitment on the part of the one making it and an expectation from the one to whom the promise is made. There are many ways in which we make promises. We may tell someone audibly that we are promising something. In conjunction with our words we may shake hands with the one to whom we are making a promise. A signed contract is another way of making a promise as is an oath in court. You might recall the unusual affirmation of a promise made by the Jews during the time of Ruth (Ruth 4:7). Perhaps different societies have offered and confirmed their promises in different ways, but the concept of a promise is timeless. When we make a promise, we are making a commitment. When we receive a promise, we are expecting the commitment to be honored.

The shortcoming of the promises that people make to one another is that sometimes individuals don't live up to their word. Granted, there could be times that circumstances prohibit one from fulfilling a promise. For instance, if one promised to mow a yard for an ill neighbor on a certain day but then had to cancel because he became ill himself that day, he would not have been able to keep the promise. Certainly he would not be at fault in that situation, but in a moment you will see the reason why this example is given. On the other hand, there are those who make promises with no intention of ever keeping them. Maybe a person just doesn't know how to say "no" to others and is thus continually overextending himself with promises that he will never have the time or resources to keep. Then again, maybe a person is just plain dishonest and makes promises with no intention of ever keeping them.

Each example given in the previous paragraph illustrates promises made and not kept. The reason they are not kept is because of human frailty. Even the first example in which the person could not fulfill a commitment because of illness is the result of human frailty. No wrong was done in that case, but, nonetheless, human frailty stood in the way of the promise going unfulfilled. This is brought out to show the contrast between the promises of men and the promises of God.

At our worst, we break promises. Even at our best, circumstances may cause us to not be able to keep our promises. God, however, has not ever, does not ever and will not ever break His promises. As the memory verse indicates, He does not lie; therefore, He does not make promises that He does not intend to keep. (Note: Some might at this point raise a question about God's conditional promises. This is a topic that is worthy of a deeper discussion. We will take this up in chapter six.) Being spirit rather than flesh (John 4:24), God is not susceptible to any type of frailty. Earthly weaknesses never hinder Him from keeping His promises. It is this rock solid foundation upon which the Christian's hope is built. God said, "For I am the Lord, I do not change..." (Malachi 3:6). James 1:17 adds, "Every good gift and every perfect gift is from above, and comes down from the Father of lights, with whom there is no variation or shadow of turning."

The words, "promise," "promises," and "promised" occur 117 times in the New King James translation of the Bible. Of those 117 occurrences, 104 refer to the promises of God.

Here are just a few passages that use the word "promise":

- I Kings 8:56 - God's promise to give Israel rest in earthly Canaan
- II Chronicles 1:9 - God's promise to David regarding the reign of his son, Solomon
- Luke 24:49; Acts 1:4 - God's promise to send the Holy Spirit upon the apostles
- Acts 2:39 - God's promise of salvation
- Romans 4:20 - God's promise to Abraham that he would have a son with Sarah
- Ephesians 6:2 - God's promise to children who honor their parents
- II Peter 3:9 - God's promise of the coming of Jesus
- I John 2:25 - God's promise of eternal life

The references just listed are only passages that use the word "promise" in them. There are many more verses that are clearly promises of God even though they do not use the word, "promise." For instance, Jesus said regarding God's daily care for us, "But seek first the kingdom of God and His righteousness, and all these things shall be added to you." (Matthew 6:33). As his life came to a close, Paul wrote of the Divine promise that he had and all faithful Christians have. "Finally, there is laid up for me the crown of righteousness, which the Lord, the righteous Judge, will give to me on that Day, and not to me only but also to all who have loved His appearing." (II Timothy 4:8). Again, the word, "promise" is not in these verses but it's obvious that a promise from God has been made.

We see hope and promise brought together a number of times in the Bible. In Acts 26:6-7, Paul spoke to Agrippa of "the hope of the promise made by God to our fathers." Whether he spoke of the promise made regarding the coming of the Messiah or the promise of the resurrection of the dead (cf. Acts 23:6), the hope is founded upon God's promise. In Ephesians 2:12, Paul wrote of the Gentiles who had been without hope and strangers from the covenant of promise. The context bears out that Paul's reference was to the time when Jew and Gentile were separated. He then went on to demonstrate that

Jesus Christ had broken down the wall that had separated the two and had brought all who obey the Gospel together through the blood of Christ (Ephesians 2:13ff). Any hope of salvation that the Gentiles could have came by virtue of God's fulfillment of His promise to send the Messiah to shed His blood. Then there is the passage which serves as this lesson's memory verse. "In hope of eternal life which God, who cannot lie, promised before time began." (Titus 1:2). While these passages use "hope" and "promise" in the same sentence, they are not the only ones that bring those two ideas together. Throughout the Bible, wherever there is hope of God's care, either in this life or the next, the foundation of that hope is the reliability of the promises of God.

What promises has God made to us today? He has promised to cleanse us of our sins when we obey His Gospel (Acts 2:38). He has promised forgiveness to us when we sin even after we become Christians if we will repent of those sins, confess them to Him and pray for forgiveness (I John 1:9; Acts 8:22). He has promised to provide for our physical needs so that we can stay focused on His kingdom and not have to worry (Matthew 6:25-34). He has promised to be by our side regardless of the challenges we might face in life (Romans 8:31-39; Hebrews 13:5). Each piece of the spiritual battle garb that He supplies carries with it the inherent promise of victory over Satan's attacks if we will put them to use (Ephesians 6:10-18). Then there are those beautiful beatitudes in Matthew 5:2-12 which promise that those who exhibit Godliness will be blessed. Finally, there is His promise of eternal life to the faithful in Christ. "And this is the promise that He has promised us - eternal life." (I John 2:25). The list of God's promises to us goes on and on. John supposed that the world could not contain all the books that could be written about the good Jesus did while He was here in the flesh (John 21:25). The same could be said for all the great promises God has made and kept throughout time.

How do we know, though, that God will keep all of these promises to us? The first way to know is by looking at His history of keeping His promises in the Bible. In Hebrews 11:1-12:3 we find an abundance of examples of God making and keeping His promises. This conclusion of this section of Scripture opens with the writer saying, "Therefore..." (Hebrews 12:1). Basically, his line of reasoning in the first three verses of Hebrews 12 is that, in order to keep from becoming discouraged by sin and giving up, we need to go back and look at history from the Word of God. When we do that, we will see that God keeps His word. Romans 8:18-39 is another series of verses that offers the same line of reasoning. Having talked about the suffering these Christians had been undergoing (verse 18), Paul asked, "What then shall we say to these things? If God is for us, who can be against us?" (Romans 8:31). Romans 8:32 in particular drives home the point that since God has a history of caring for His people, He will care for us as well. "He who did not spare His own Son, but delivered Him up for us all, how shall He not with Him also freely give us all things?" God showed how much He loves us and how faithful He is to His promises in that He sent Jesus to die for us. If He kept that tremendous promise, will He not also keep His daily promises to us?

The second way we know that God will keep His promises to us is by looking at our own history. Whether you pause in your reading at this point or wait until you have finished this chapter, would you please take some time to look back over your life and think of specific examples of how God has fulfilled the promises that He has made to you through His written Word? Take as much time as you like doing this but you probably won't have to search much further back than this very day or even this very moment. Look around you at your physical blessings. Those are from God (James 1:17) and are fulfillments of His promise (Matthew 6:33). Consider the hope of heaven that you have if you are a faithful Christian. That is from God and is the fulfillment of His promise (Titus 1:2). Have you, as a Christian, sinned today or in previous days? Did you pray for forgiveness? That blessing of cleansing is from God and is the fulfillment of His promise (I John 1:7-9). In life's trials, have you felt the peace that surpasses all understanding as the result of offering prayer and supplication with thanksgiving (Philippians 4:6-7)? God gave you the blessing of prayer and the peace that results from it is the fulfillment of His promise. Feel free to add to this list as you review your life. In fact, why not make this a daily practice so that you never forget God's care for you?

One of the reasons we lose hope is because we forget. The church in Ephesus left their first love (Revelation 2:4). They had forgotten God and were told to remember (Revelation 2:5).

Why do we forget? Would the phrase, "out of sight, out of mind" apply here? When we block God's Word as well as how good He has been to us from our memory, we will lose hope because we will forget how faithful and rock solid He is (Psalm 18:2). God IS faithful (Romans 3:4; I Corinthians 1:9; 10:13; II Timothy 2:13). His promises prompted hope in the faithful men and women of old. You yourself have seen that hope in the lives of Christians who have influenced you. You yourself have experienced that hope. Even though you can enjoy the hope built on God's promises at this moment in your life, your hope can grow stronger and deeper.

God's promises are certain. God's promises are sure. God's promises are firm because they are HIS promises and His promises never fail. That it is impossible for Him to lie is an unalterable truth (Hebrews 6:18). His "exceedingly great and precious promises" (II Peter 1:4) are why the Christian can face every challenge, every trial, and every temptation with hope.

EXERCISE YOUR MIND

True or False

1. Promises made by men and women are sometimes broken. T   F

2. God does not lie. □ T □ F
3. Spiritual hope is founded upon the promises of God. □ T □ F
4. All blessings are from God. □ T □ F
5. One of the reasons we lose hope is because we neglect to study God's Word. □ T □ F

Multiple Choice

1. A promise is:
   A) made to be broken;
   B) a very precious item;
   C) not very important.

2. Faithful Christians can have hope in God's promise of eternal life because:
   A) their feelings are guiding them;
   B) a preacher said they can;
   C) God cannot lie.

3. Hope and promise:
   A) are brought together a number of times in the Bible;
   B) are never used together;
   C) are polar opposites.

4. God blesses us:
   A) on rare occasions;
   B) daily;
   C) when it is convenient for Him.

5. Hope:
   A) can grow stronger and deeper;
   B) can never grow;
   C) is impossible to obtain.

Fill in the Blanks

(Note: All scripture quotations are taken from the New King James Version and can be found in this lesson.)

1. "Every good _____ and every perfect _____ is from _____, and comes down from the _____ of lights, with whom there is no _____ or shadow of _____."
2. "But seek _____ the _____ of God and His _____, and all these things shall be _____ to you."
3. "Finally, there is laid up for me the _____ of righteousness, which the _____, the righteous _____, will give to me on that _____, and not to me only but also to all who have _____ His appearing."
4. "And this is the _____ that He has promised us _____."
5. "He who did not _____ His own _____, but _____ Him up for us all, how shall He not with Him also _____ give us all things?"

Questions for Discussion

1. How do we feel when someone breaks a promise to us? _____
   _____
   _____
   _____

2. What are some other reasons why someone might break his or her promise? _____
   _____
   _____
   _____

Hope's Firm Foundation

3. In what ways are God's promises superior to the promises that we humans make? _____

_____

_____

_____

4. What promise of God is most memorable to you? Cite Bible book, chapter and verse for the promise and tell why it is so memorable. _____

_____

_____

_____

5. What did the Lord mean when He said that He "does not change" (Malachi 3:6)? _____

_____

_____

_____

6. What is the meaning of Romans 8:31-32? _____

_____

_____

_____

7. Why is Romans 8:38-39 such an encouraging passage? _____

_____

_____

_____

8. Using a good concordance, find at least one other verse that uses the word "promise" as it relates to a promise God has made to mankind and explain its meaning. _____

_____

_____

_____

9. Why is it important for us to trust God's promise that He will provide for our physical needs? _____

_____

_____

_____

10. What are some of the eternal blessings that God has promised the faithful in heaven? Be sure to give scripture references. _____

_____

_____

_____

11. Have you ever felt that you had no hope? Assuming that you are more hopeful now, what did you do to build your hope?

_____

_____

_____

12. Why does Satan want us to give up hope? _____

_____

_____

_____

13. Name at least one of the promises that God has made in His Word and has kept or is keeping in your life. _____
_____
_____
_____

14. What do we allow to cause us to forget God? _____
_____
_____
_____

15. What are some ways in which we can keep from forgetting God?
_____
_____
_____

SEARCH THE SCRIPTURES

(Note: For this section, you will find a good concordance helpful. All scripture quotations are taken from the New King James Version.)

Where is the following Bible verse located? _____

"Uphold me according to Your word, that I may live; And do not let me be ashamed of my hope."

Chapter Three

Hope's Partners in the Heart

Memory Work:

"But let us who are of the day be sober, putting on the breastplate of faith and love, and *as* a helmet the hope of salvation." (I Thessalonians 5:8)

Hope, just by itself, can bring joy to our lives. The Psalmist wrote, "Happy *is he* who *has* the God of Jacob for his help, whose hope *is* in the LORD his God." (Psalm 146:5). Jeremiah added, "Blessed *is* the man who trusts in the LORD, And whose hope is the LORD." (Jeremiah 17:7). But hope is not alone in its service to faithful Christians. It has two powerful partners that, working together, can lead us to heaven.

I Corinthians 13:13 is probably the best known of the passages that reference this tremendous triad. Paul wrote, "And now abide faith, hope, love, these three; but the greatest of these *is* love." The fact that these three abide with the faithful Christian indicates that they are constant companions of the one who is traveling on heaven's road. They are like the friends who never leave us through thick or thin. Each works together to lead us on our journey to eternal life. Faith provides the firm foundation we need in order to stand when the winds of trial and temptation blow (II Corinthians 1:24). Hope produces optimism that there is reward for our faithfulness (Romans 8:24-28). Love generates within us an unselfish, service-minded attitude that focuses on others rather than on ourselves (I Corinthians 13:5).

Faith, hope, and love abide. They are ever present in this world. They abide because their source, God Himself, abides. II Timothy 2:13 says, "If we are faithless, He remains faithful; He cannot deny Himself." Furthermore, the written Word that He inspired to direct our faith, hope, and love abides (I Peter 1:23). When we cannot find faith, hope, and love, it is not because they have left us. It is because we have left them. Like God and His Word, they are readily available to aid us in our daily walk. In fact, they are found by seeking God through His Word.

Peter wrote that God's Divine power has "given to us all things that *pertain* to life and godliness, through the knowledge of Him who called us by glory and virtue." (II Peter 1:3). The Lord has given us what we need to sustain our faith, hope, and love. We need not worry that He is going to suddenly take them away while this earth stands. They abide. It us up to us to cling tenaciously to them and grow in them.

Another passage that notes hope's partners in the heart is Colossians 1:3-5. Paul wrote, "We give thanks to the God and Father of our Lord Jesus Christ, praying always for you, since we heard of your faith in Christ Jesus and of your love for all the saints; because of the hope which is laid up for you in heaven, of which you heard before in the word of the truth of the gospel."

In this passage, hope is portrayed as a motivating factor for faith and love. Why do we keep building our faith through study of God's Word? Why do we strive to grow in love? Other verses may add reasons, but in this context, the reason is our hope of heaven.

Have you ever been challenged in your faith? Perhaps some tragedy occurred in your life and you questioned why God would allow you to experience such suffering. Perhaps someone belittled you for your belief in God, causing you to wonder about His existence. There are many ways that our faith can be challenged, each of which is capable of disturbing us and causing us to be become discouraged. In Psalm 42 we find the Psalmist in a faith-challenging situation. He had been seeking God and, while so doing, had become the subject of ridicule (Psalm 42:3). He looked at his situation, then he looked up to God in faith and said to himself, " Why are you cast down, O my soul? And *why* are you disquieted within me? Hope in God, for I shall yet praise Him *for* the help of His countenance." (Psalm 42:5). He essentially repeated his words in Psalm 42:11 and Psalm 43:5. He knew by faith that God was with him. He needed to remind himself to continue to have hope that God would hear his pleas. His hope and faith worked together to lift him up.

Have you ever felt like not loving? The examples in the preceding paragraph could be given here as well. Perhaps a tragedy in your life was caused by another person and it became difficult for you to love them because of it. Being belittled by someone would certainly have been a challenge to your ability to love them. Jesus said, "But I say to you, love your enemies, bless those who curse you, do good to those who hate you, and pray for those who spitefully use you and persecute you." (Matthew 5:44). How can we love those who abuse us? The answer lies in the hope of heaven that we have in our hearts. We endure the mistreatment because we know that in eternity we will have a dwelling in which nothing evil shall harm us (Revelation 21:27). We weather the abuse and seek to show love because our hope has our thoughts in heaven (Colossians 3:1-2). We also do this because we want to see those souls in heaven. Hatred will not lead them to God. They need to see the hope that is in us (I Peter 3:15). They will see this hope when we show them our love.

Notice how Colossians 1:5 closes with the fact that the Word of God is the source of the hope that motivates faith and love. The way to grow in faith, hope, and love is through God's Word. The Bible is the source of faith (Romans 10:17), we learn of the hope of heaven from the Bible (I Peter 1:3-5), and, in the Bible, we are taught how to love (John 13:34).

Faith, hope, and love are again mentioned together in I Thessalonians 1:3. Paul wrote, "Remembering without ceasing your work of faith, labor of love, and patience of hope in our Lord Jesus Christ in the sight of our God and Father." Here we see that the three are combined with effort on the part of those who possess them. Three different Greek words are used for "work," "labor," and "patience," but each indicates activity. While we clearly understand the active nature of the words, "work" and "labor," we typically think of patience as being inactive. We might believe that patience is little more than just sitting around waiting for something to happen. That, however, is not how the Bible describes patience. James exhorted, "But let patience have *its* perfect work, that you may be perfect and complete, lacking nothing." (James 1:4). Patience is industrious rather than indolent. Patience works.

Having clarified the active nature of patience, we now note how each of these actions (work, labor, and patience) ties in with faith, hope, and love. Faith, hope, and love each serve to motivate action. They are not dormant.

The Thessalonian Christians were being commended by Paul. He had seen their faith through their works. This reminds us of the words of James in James 2:18. "But someone will say, 'You have faith, and I have works.' Show me your faith without your works, and I will show you my faith by my works." In I Thessalonians 1:8 we find a reference to these Christians' work for the Lord. "For from you the word of the Lord has sounded forth, not only in Macedonia and Achaia, but also in every place. Your faith toward God has gone out, so that we do not need to say anything."

Paul had seen their love through their labors. Later in this epistle he wrote, "But concerning brotherly love you have no need that I should write to you, for you yourselves are taught by God to love one another; and indeed you do so toward all the brethren who are in all Macedonia. But we urge you, brethren, that you increase more and more." (I Thessalonians 4:9-10).

He had seen their hope through their patience. Twice in the epistle Paul spoke of the affliction and suffering these children of God patiently endured for the cause of Christ. "And you became followers of us and of the Lord, having received the word in much affliction, with joy of the Holy Spirit." (I Thessalonians 1:6). "For you, brethren, became imitators of the churches of God which are in Judea in Christ Jesus. For you also suffered the same things from your own countrymen, just as they *did* from the Judeans." (I Thessalonians 2:14).

Faith, hope, and love work. Of course, we are the ones who implement them. God makes them available to us. It is up to us to utilize them.

Another passage that combines faith, hope, and love is this chapter's memory verse. "But let us who are of the day be sober, putting on the breastplate of faith and love, and *as* a helmet the hope of salvation." (I Thessalonians 5:8). Reminiscent of Paul's more detailed description of the spiritual armor in Ephesians 6:11-17, this verse presents faith, hope, and love as defensive tools against Satan's attacks. From a physical standpoint, the heart and the head are two of the most vulnerable locations on our bodies. In Paul's day, a breastplate was worn to protect the chest area, including the heart, while the helmet, of course, was worn to protect the head. Spiritually speaking, with the heart representing the very depths of one's being and the head representing the mind, we know that these are also extremely vulnerable. Faith and love protect the heart while hope protects the mind.

The importance of faith, hope, and love working together in defense against the devil's efforts is clearly seen in these military images. Which piece of physical battle gear do you think the solider in Paul's day would have been willing to leave behind? Would he consciously decide to protect his heart with the breastplate but leave the helmet on the shelf? Would he do the opposite and cover his head with the helmet while neglecting to shield his heart?

It's easy for us to understand why a soldier would want as much protection as he could get in battle. Why would a Christian not want the same in the spiritual war? Which of these would you want to leave out of your life: Faith? Hope? Love? Together, the three come to our aid when we are engaged in combat with the evils of the world. Faith protects us as it reminds us through God's Word that the Lord is still with us, even in the heat of trial. "I will never leave you nor forsake you." (Hebrews 13:5). Love is our defense against a desire to take vengeance on those who attack us. "Repay no one evil for evil. Have regard for good things in the sight of all men." (Romans 12:17). Hope is the positive outlook that channels our thoughts toward the spiritual blessings that we, as Christians, enjoy in Christ when the world tries to drag our minds down into the depths of despair. The Lord even gave us a list of positive thoughts to keep our minds and our hope up. "Finally, brethren, whatever things are true, whatever things *are* noble, whatever things *are* just, whatever things *are* pure, whatever things *are* lovely, whatever things *are* of good report, if *there is* any virtue and if *there is* anything praiseworthy—meditate on these things." (Philippians 4:8).

We can't help but see in this passage a point that has already been made regarding the effectiveness of faith, hope, and love in our lives. Paul said that we are to put on the protective gear. Neither a breastplate nor a helmet would have magically appeared on a soldier as he faced down the enemy. He would have had to make the effort to put each item on his body. So it is with this spiritual equipment. We must put faith, hope, and love into our hearts and minds and we must keep them on. The moment that we become lax is the moment that we open ourselves up to injury from Satan's weapons. Faith, hope, and love can protect us, but if we neglect to put them on, keep them on, and get stronger in them each day, they will be of little value to us. Thanks be unto God for His powerful, inspired Word, the Bible, that fully equips us with the tools we need to fend off the enemy.

Hope, faith, and love, are tremendous blessings from God. As we have seen in this lesson, these three abide, being here with us and for us (I Corinthians 13:13). These three sustain us as hope motivates faith and love (Colossians 1:3-5). These three work in our lives when we avail ourselves of them (I Thessalonians 1:3). These three protect us as we battle with Satan (I Thessalonians 5:8).

In chapter four we will consider the tragedy of a life lived without hope. Imagine here for just a moment what this world would be like if not just hope, but also faith and love were absent. It's depressing just to think about it. No one would be doing anything to help anyone else. Each person would be "looking out for number one." There would be no reason for optimism. Every tragedy would be cause for despair. Getting older would be nothing more than getting one step closer to the grave. Life would be a ritual, devoid of enthusiasm and joy. That's what a world without faith, hope, and love, a world without God, would be like.

Now let's ponder a world in which faith, hope, and love dominate. There would be more people helping each other because love would be prevalent. There would be optimism, even in the midst of tragedy, because hope of being in the eternal land where there is no sadness would abound. There would be meaning in every day as faith of God's abiding presence would rule the human heart.

In which of these worlds would you rather live? The fact of the matter is that people are living in each of these worlds right now. Those who are away from God live in the first world while those who are walking with God live in the second. As long as this earth stands, these two worlds will exist. However, as Christians, we can lead those in the world of sadness into the world of light by teaching them the Gospel of Jesus Christ and showing them our faith, hope, and love. May we ever remember that these blessings we enjoy are not for us to hoard, but to share.

> "You are the salt of the earth; but if the salt loses its flavor, how shall it be seasoned? It is then good for nothing but to be thrown out and trampled underfoot by men. You are the light of the world. A city that is set on a hill cannot be hidden. Nor do they light a lamp and put it under a basket, but on a lampstand, and it gives light to all *who are* in the house. Let your light so shine before men, that they may see your good works and glorify your Father in heaven." (Matthew 5:13-16).

EXERCISE YOUR MIND

True or False

1. Faith, hope, and love work together to lead us on our journey to eternal life. T F
2. We develop faith, hope, and love through the study of God's Word. T F
3. Hope motivates faith and love. T F
4. Faith, hope, and love are of no value to us in our battle with Satan. T F
5. There are lost people in the world who need the Gospel of Jesus Christ. T F

Multiple Choice

1. Faith provides:
   A) little help to us;
   B) the firm foundation we need in order to stand when the winds of trial and temptation blow;
   C) no help at all to us.

2. Hope produces:
   A) optimism;
   B) pessimism;
   C) skepticism.

3. Love generates within us:
   A) apathy;
   B) an unselfish, service-minded attitude;
   C) self-centeredness.

4. We can be encouraged by:
   A) looking to God in faith;

B) not thinking about God;
C) thinking about how God will take vengeance on the disobedient.
5. The people around us need to see:
A) our lack of concern for serving God;
B) our lack of concern for their souls;
C) our faith, hope, and love.

Fill in the Blanks

(Note: All scripture quotations are taken from the New King James Version and can be found in this lesson.)
1. "_____ *is he* who *has* the _____ of Jacob for his _____, whose _____ *is* in the LORD his God."
2. "And now abide _____, _____, _____, these three; but the _____ of these *is* love."
3. "We give _____ to the _____ and _____ of our Lord Jesus Christ, _____ always for you, since we heard of your _____ in Christ Jesus and of your _____ for all the saints; because of the _____ which is laid up for you in _____, of which you heard before in the _____ of the _____ of the _____."
4. "_____ without _____ your _____ of faith, _____ of love, and _____ of hope in our Lord Jesus Christ in the sight of our _____ and _____."
5. "Repay no one _____ for _____. Have regard for _____ things in the _____ of all men."

Questions for Discussion

1. In what ways can we demonstrate our hope? _____

_____

_____

2. In what ways can we demonstrate our love? _____

_____

_____

_____

3. In what ways can we demonstrate our faith? _____

_____

_____

_____

4. What are some things that happen to us in life that can challenge our faith? _____

_____

_____

_____

5. What is the best way to respond to a person who challenges our faith? _____

_____

_____

_____

6. What is the best way to respond to a person who treats us in an unloving manner? _____

_____

Hope's Partners in the Heart 33

7. How would a non-Christian be affected by seeing evidence of our hope? _____

8. How would it help fellow Christians to see our hope? _____

9. How does patience "work"? _____

10. Why do our hearts and minds need to be protected? _____

11. In what ways does Satan attack our hearts and minds? _____

12. How do the thoughts noted in Philippians 4:8 build hope within us? _____

13. Select one of the thoughts listed in Philippians 4:8 and give an example of it (e.g., what is something "true" about which we can think?). _____
   _____
   _____
   _____

14. Why must we "put on" the breastplate of faith and love and the helmet of the hope of salvation? _____
   _____
   _____
   _____

15. Why is it important for us to study the Bible to build our faith, hope, and love? _____
   _____
   _____
   _____

SEARCH THE SCRIPTURES

(Note: For this section, you will find a good concordance helpful. All scripture quotations are taken from the New King James Version.)

Where is the following Bible verse located? *Col 1:23*

"If indeed you continue in the faith, grounded and steadfast, and are not moved away from the hope of the gospel which you heard, which was preached to every creature under heaven, of which I, Paul, became a minister."

Chapter Four

"Abandon Hope - All Ye Who Enter Here"

Memory Work:

"And they said, 'That is hopeless! So we will walk according to our own plans, and we will every one obey the dictates of his evil heart.'" (Jeremiah 18:12)

The title of this chapter comes from Dante Alighieri's well known 14th century poem, "Divine Comedy." Entitled, "Inferno," the first part of the poem chronicles Dante's "journey" through hell. As he approached the gate of hell he noticed a sign which read, "Abandon Hope - All Ye Who Enter Here." Based on the Bible's depiction of hell, this would seem to be a most appropriate message greeting those who die in their sins. The rich man who would not help Lazarus certainly found the hopelessness of hell to be real (Luke 16:19-31). Searching for just a single moment of relief, he was told, "Son, remember that in your lifetime you received your good things, and likewise Lazarus evil things; but now he is comforted and you are tormented." (Luke 16:25). Any hope he might have found on earth disappeared upon his death. This account of the rich man's feelings of hopelessness parallel a statement that king Solomon had made centuries earlier. "When a wicked man dies, *his* expectation will perish, and the hope of the unjust perishes." (Proverbs 11:7).

It may seem strange to some that a book about hope would contain a chapter about hopelessness. Some might even choose to simply skim this chapter or avoid it completely out of their distaste for anything "negative." The reason this chapter exists is due to my longstanding belief that Christians can have a greater appreciation for God when we more fully comprehend where we would be without Him.

In Luke 7:36-50, we read about Jesus visiting in the home of Simon the Pharisee. Knowing where Jesus was, a sinful woman came in and washed the Lord's feet with her tears and dried them with her hair. She then proceeded to kiss His feet and anoint them with precious ointment. Simon was amazed that Jesus allowed this "horrible" woman to even touch Him. Having read Simon's thoughts, Jesus told him a story about two men who owed money. One owed a considerable sum while the other owed just a small amount. In Jesus' story, both men were forgiven of their debt. Jesus asked Simon which of those two debtors would be the most appreciative for the forgiveness of the debt. Simon accurately responded that the one who had owed more would be the most thankful. From there, Jesus went on to make the application of His story. Simon had given Jesus a minimal welcome while the woman had lavished Him with attention. What's more, her attentiveness was couched in her recognition of both her sinfulness and the greatness of Jesus. Verse 47 is pertinent to the statement made in the previous paragraph about appreciating God. Jesus said, "Therefore I say to you, her sins, which *are* many, are forgiven, for she loved much. But to whom little is forgiven, *the same* loves little." The woman knew where she was without the Lord. She knew how empty a life in pursuit of sin could be. Her reflection on a sinful life of hopelessness made her love and appreciate Jesus for the redemption and hope that He offered.

Let's think, then, for a few minutes about a life without God. First and foremost, without Him, there is no salvation. God said through Isaiah, "Look to Me, and be saved, All you ends of the earth! For I *am* God, and *there is* no other." (Isaiah 45:22). Paul wrote that God is the Savior of all mankind, especially those who believe (I Timothy 4:10). Peter said that there is no salvation outside of Jesus Christ (Acts 4:12), a statement that has been true ever since the establishment of the Lord's church in the first century A.D. (Acts 2).

Without salvation, we would still be in our sins and, thus, separated from God (Isaiah 59:1,2). We would have to remain shackled to the guilt and shame of sin (Romans 6:16). We would cry out with Paul, "O wretched man that I am! Who will deliver me from this body of death?" (Romans 7:24), and there would be no one there to answer. There would be no one there to deliver us.

Without salvation, we would have nothing to which we could look forward after death. We would wake up each morning with the realization that this day, like the day before, and each one to come, would be just another day closer to death.

Without salvation, there would be no real joy, no abiding peace, and no firm hope. Life would be miserable as we would see both ourselves and those around us slowly but surely marching on toward life's end.

At this point, someone who does not believe in God might object. They might contend that they are peaceful and happy. The question for those individuals is, "What is the basis of your peace and happiness?" If the basis is not God, then it is temporal, and anything that is temporal is going to pass away. If we base our happiness on other people, we will be disappointed because people can hurt us and even the most faithful of friends can die, leaving us without the reason for our happiness. If we base our happiness on things, we will be disappointed because things wear out. Even if we base our happiness on ourselves, we will be disappointed because we fail so often and our lives are going to come to an end.

Perhaps an even better question for those who choose to live lives away from God is, "What hope do you have?" Again, all of the responses will be worldly and temporal. Some might express hope for a nice house, a family, a comfortable retirement, etc., but each of these hopes is short-lived because their foundations are temporal. They just will not last. What real, long-lasting hope do those who do not follow God really have? The best they can answer is a cross-your-fingers, wishing type of hope that if there is a God, maybe He will be merciful in the end. That is not real hope. It is uncertainty and it cannot sustain one through life's ups and downs.

Paul referenced this hopeless life when he wrote his first letter to the Thessalonian congregation of the Lord's church. The Christians there were concerned about their loved ones who had died in the Lord. Paul reassured them that if they remained faithful to God, they would see their saved loved ones again (I Thessalonians 4:13-18). Note his words as he began this exhortation. "But I do not want you to be ignorant, brethren, concerning those who have fallen asleep, lest you sorrow as others who have no hope." (I Thessalonians 4:13). The last part of that sentence sums up a life lived without God in it. It's a life of sorrow. The Christians to whom Paul was writing could have hope because of their faith that the Lord would come in judgment and eternally save them and their fellow faithful spiritual brothers and sisters. Non-Christians can only look forward to the end of this life in sadness and grief. Isaiah wrote, "For Sheol cannot thank You, Death cannot praise You; Those who go down to the pit cannot hope for Your truth." (Isaiah 38:18).

Not only does a life without God mean no salvation, it also leads to a tragic frame of mind. Can there be anything more depressing than an atheist's view of life? To an atheist, each of us is nothing more than a haphazard gathering of particles whose origin is a slimy, primordial ooze. We are not in the image of God but instead are the product of a single-cell amoeba, multiple mutations, and a chain of links of monkey-men (one of which is still "missing," by the way).

How can there be any true appreciation for life or love in the atheist's heart? An atheist might respond, "But I do appreciate life and love," and yet he or she is at a loss to explain why. If we are indeed the product of "the survival of the fittest," then our natural instinct should be to destroy those who are weaker so that they don't interfere with those who are stronger.

What is the origin of an appreciation for life, love, and all of the other glories of this life? The origin is, of course, God, even though one may refuse to admit His existence. God is still here, even if all of us were to deny His presence. His existence is not based on our belief (Romans 3:3-4). He is not a Freudian illusion. But take the acknowledgement of God's presence away from your heart and you have little choice but to view life as random and purposeless. Life becomes a throwaway.

A life without God produces a self-serving society. Who or what is the ultimate standard of right and wrong without God? Some would argue that the "greater good" would rule. Thus, we would have laws against stealing, murder, etc. because they would exist so that the greatest number of people could be happy. But without God, why is one person's happiness more important than another's? If one wants something that another has or if one wants to eliminate someone who he or she does not like, on what basis would that be wrong without God as the standard? Those who are even marginally acquainted with history recall a man named Hitler who felt that there was nothing wrong with stealing and with murdering those whom he considered inferior. God said that we should not steal or murder (Romans 13:9). Without Him as the standard, though, we have no right to condemn a man or even an entire country when they decide to follow the way that they think is right. Their views and ours would be equally acceptable. If not, why not?

Life without God means no salvation. It means a tragic frame of mind. It means a society of self-serving individuals. How could anyone possibly have hope in a world like that?! It's no wonder that there is so much sadness in this world. The irony is that this sadness is so very unnecessary. Those who are going through this life without hope do not need to do so. God is here and He offers hope.

As Paul traveled by ship to Rome, he was able to see first-hand what hopelessness looked like. The storms were battering the ship to the point that Luke said all hope that they should be saved had disappeared (Acts 27:20). In contrast to the majority on the ship who had given up, Paul looked up to God and confidently spoke of His care for all who were aboard. His powerful statement recorded in Acts 27:25 rings true even today in hearts of hope. "Therefore take heart, men, for I believe God that it will be just as it was told me." Paul refused to get caught up in the hopelessness and despair and chose instead to turn to God, the source of hope. As we read on, we see that Paul's hope in God inspired hope even in those who had once themselves felt hopeless.

As Christians, may we thank God every day for what He has done in delivering us from the life of hopelessness through our obedience to His Gospel. May we shine the light of Christ so that those who are still hopeless can see the brightness of salvation and the shining glory of the blessings that God abundantly provides for us on a daily basis.

This chapter closes with an appeal to Christians who have chosen to go back into the world. Paul wrote of brother Demas who, having once loved and obeyed God, fell back in love with the world and its hopeless ways (II Timothy 4:10). Peter wrote of the terrifying eternity that awaits Christians who fall away and go back to lives of sin (II Peter 2:20-22).

Dear Christian friend, do you not remember what life was like before you obeyed the Gospel of Jesus Christ? Have you forgotten the hopelessness that shrouded your daily walk when you were separated from God? All of the aspects of hopelessness that have been cited in this chapter once characterized your life. Then you heard God's Word (Romans 10:17), you believed on Jesus as the Christ (John 8:24), you repented of your sins (Luke 13:3), you confessed your faith in Jesus as the Christ (Romans 10:10), and you were immersed into Christ for the forgiveness of your sins (Acts 2:38). You rose up from the waters of immersion as a new creature (II Corinthians 5:17) with all of your past sins taken away by the blood of Christ (Romans 6:1-7). God blessed you on that day of your salvation and He has blessed you every day since, even if you are now not acknowledging His care for you. Why did you want to go back to the life that offers only fleeting pleasures? Why did you desert the only One who gives true and lasting hope? There is absolutely nothing in this world that is worth losing your soul for.

Just as non-Christians do not have to stay in their hopelessness, Christians who have gone back into the world of sin do not have to remain hopeless either. Peter told the erring Christian, Simon, that he could repent of his sins and pray for forgiveness (Acts 8:22). You can do the same.

It is sad beyond words when people choose to abandon the hope that God offers by turning away from Him. Thankfully, God is patient (II Peter 3:9). May all avail themselves of the blessed hope that He offers through obedience to His Word.

EXERCISE YOUR MIND

True or False

1. We can have a greater appreciation for God when we more fully comprehend where we would be without Him. T F
2. It's possible for us to take God's blessings for granted. T F
3. Without God, there is no salvation. T F
4. We can have true peace even if we don't follow God. T F
5. Both heaven and hell are real. T F

Multiple Choice

1. The rich man reminds us that:
   A) life is short so we should get all the wealth we can while we can get it;
   B) we should not care for the poor;
   C) after death, we cannot change where we are in eternity.

2. The woman who washed Jesus' feet:
   A) appreciated both her own sinfulness and Jesus' greatness;
   B) was just putting on a show to get attention;
   C) was ignored by Jesus.

3. Today, salvation can be found:
   A) only in Jesus Christ;
   B) in Islam;
   C) in Judaism.

4. Without God:
   A) each person's standard for right and wrong would be acceptable;
   B) we would have no right condemn someone as long as they think they are right;
   C) both A and B.

5. A Christian who falls away from God and goes back into the world:
   A) is still saved;
   B) is in danger of eternal punishment;
   C) is setting a great example for those who want to go to heaven.

Fill in the Blanks

(Note: All scripture quotations are taken from the New King James Version and can be found in this lesson.)

1. "Son, _____ that in your _____ you received your _____ things, and likewise Lazarus _____ things; but now he is _____ and you are _____."
2. "Therefore I say to you, her _____, which *are* many, are _____, for she loved much. But to whom little is _____, *the same* loves _____."
3. "Look to _____, and be _____, All you ends of the _____! For I *am* _____, and *there is* no _____."

4. "O _____ man that I am! Who will _____ me from this body of _____?"
5. "For _____ cannot thank You, _____ cannot _____ You; Those who go down to the _____ cannot _____ for Your _____."

Questions for Discussion

1. Name one characteristic of hell that is given us in the Bible.

2. Why is there no hope in hell?

3. What is the danger in not acknowledging the existence of hell?

4. How does realizing what God has saved us help us appreciate salvation?

5. Why would one forgiven of a large debt be more appreciative than one forgiven of a small debt? _____

_____

_____

_____

6. What is the meaning of Jesus' statement in Matthew 9:12?

_____

_____

_____

7. Name some of the "gods" to which people turn instead of the one true God about whom we read in the Bible. _____

_____

_____

_____

8. What are some of the "things" of this world to which people turn in an effort to find happiness? _____

_____

_____

_____

9. Name any other reasons that come to mind as to why a life without God is a life of hopelessness. _____

_____

_____

_____

"Abandon Hope - All Ye Who Enter Here"

10. Should a faithful Christian be looking forward to the Lord's coming in judgment? Explain your answer. _____
_____
_____
_____

11. Give one example of the evil influence that atheistic thinking has had on our society. _____
_____
_____
_____

12. Where do we get our desire to help others? _____
_____
_____
_____

13. What can Christians do to help those who are hopeless? _____
_____
_____
_____

14. Why is it dangerous for a Christian to turn away from God and go back into the world? _____
_____
_____
_____

15. At what point should we give up hope? _____

_____

_____

_____

SEARCH THE SCRIPTURES

(Note: For this section, you will find a good concordance helpful. All scripture quotations are taken from the New King James Version.)

Where is the following Bible verse located? _____

"That at that time you were without Christ, being aliens from the commonwealth of Israel and strangers from the covenants of promise, having no hope and without God in the world."

Chapter Five

In Defense of Hope

Memory Work:

"But sanctify the Lord God in your hearts, and always *be* ready to *give* a defense to everyone who asks you a reason for the hope that is in you, with meekness and fear." (I Peter 3:15)

The Christians to whom Peter originally wrote his first epistle were experiencing severe persecution for their faith. I Peter 1:7 in the King James Version speaks of "the trial of your faith" and being "tried with fire." I Peter 2:20, 4:1, 4:16, and 4:19 each reference suffering. 3:9 mentions evil and reviling. 4:14 speaks of being reproached for the name of Christ. In 4:12, the words, "fiery trial" are used. Ensuing verses seem to suggest that the suffering would intensify.

The letter is filled with Peter's words of encouragement to these children of God to remain strong and continue in their faithfulness. Among his words of exhortation are some that are well known to most Christians still today. They are the words of I Peter 3:15, the passage that is this chapter's memory verse.

The Greek word translated, "ready" can also be translated, "prepared." Some English versions render it that way. Even though this is a single word, its different translations present some interesting insights. Being ready indicates a determination to give a defense of hope. "I'm ready and am always looking for the opportunity to tell someone about Jesus Christ, the source of my hope." Being prepared denotes study has been done and conviction is in the heart. "I'm prepared with firm answers for those who ask me about my hope." Together the two translations portray a word that demonstrates both a preparation for and a willingness to give a defense of the hope that is in the Christian heart. Preparation without determination will keep us silent. We will know why we have hope but we will not tell others. Determination without preparation will cause us to speak, but we will speak in error if we don't know the Word that is the source of our hope.

When we look at this verse, we might be tempted to think that Peter is only telling us to be able to quote book, chapter and verse whenever someone challenges our beliefs. Indeed, we should be able to reference scriptures but so much more can be gained from our readiness and preparedness to give a defense.

According to the opening words of I Peter 3:15, the defense of our hope begins with us sanctifying God in our hearts. This means that we set Him apart, giving Him the highest priority. Paul wrote, "If then you were raised with Christ, seek those things which are above, where Christ is, sitting at the right hand of God. Set your mind on things above, not on things on the earth." (Colossians 3:1-2). By sanctifying God in our hearts, we are focusing on Him. It is this focus that not only prepares us to give a defense, but also makes us stronger spiritually. Thus, we benefit personally when we prepare ourselves to defend our hope.

How well do we know the Word of God? Several years ago when I was working at a radio station in West Tennessee, I came across a magazine published by an atheist organization. One of the comments that a writer made has stuck with me after all this time. He said, "We atheists have the upper hand. Most Christians only know Psalm 23 and John 3:16. Beyond that, they cannot defend what they claim to believe." Is this true?

Paul wrote, "Be diligent to present yourself approved to God, a worker who does not need to be ashamed, rightly dividing the word of truth." (II Timothy 2:15). Is daily study of God's Word a part of your life? Are you building spiritual muscle and strengthening your faith each day? Do you desire the pure milk of the Word like a newborn baby desires milk (I Peter 2:2)?

In the days of Hosea, God said through the mighty prophet that Israel was destroyed for a lack of knowledge (Hosea 4:6). Before Israel entered into the earthly promised land of Canaan, they were warned several times by Moses that they should not forget God and that they should obey His Word (Deuteronomy 4:23; 6:12; 8:11; et al.). According to the author of the book of Judges, after a period of time in the earthly promised land of Canaan, Israel "forsook the Lord God of their fathers, who had brought them out of the land of Egypt; and they followed other gods from *among* the gods of the people who *were* all around them, and they bowed down to them; and they provoked the Lord to anger." (Judges 2:12). They had been warned not to forget God. As they forgot Him, they forsook Him and as they forsook Him they knew less and less about Him. They allowed themselves to be woven into the fabric of an evil society and simply became like the world. Some remained faithful to God, but many did not. After awhile, it was difficult to tell the difference between the wicked inhabitants of Canaan and those whom God had led to that place. They had no distinctiveness and they had no hope for they had forsaken the God of hope (Romans 15:13). They no longer knew Him. They were destroyed for a lack of knowledge.

What is the state of what the world calls Christianity today? For all intents and purposes, it appears to be a hodgepodge of doctrines and creeds authored by a god who is too confused to provide His followers with a credible, single source of direction. In reality, God has given mankind His perfect Word which is able to guide us toward eternity (II Timothy 3:16-17; II Peter 1:3). Sadly, our neglect of His Word in favor of the doctrines and traditions of men has produced the religious confusion. In turn, many find it difficult to defend the hope that God offers because they do not study and grow in the source of that hope, choosing instead to occupy their minds with the words of mere men.

While some have chosen to rely on the words of men, others have made the decision to trust their feelings as their source of hope. When asked why they hope in God, these individuals will reply with statements like, "I just feel His presence" or, "I feel that I am doing what is right." Feelings are real and feelings are involved in our walk with God, but they are inadequate as a defense of our hope. The non-believer could just as easily respond that he feels God does not exist. He would claim that his feelings would be just as viable as the Christian's feelings and he would be correct. There has to be something more than feelings upon which to found our hope.

God's Word is the source for building our hope. When we realize that, we will spend more time reading it, meditating upon it, and incorporating it into our lives. Doing that, we will be better able to give concrete evidence for our hope. "Why do you believe in God?" the atheist will ask. "Because, 'since the creation of the world His invisible *attributes* are clearly seen,'" you might answer. (Romans 1:20). "Why do you believe that Jesus Christ is the Savior?" another will ask. "Because He is the fulfillment of every Old Testament prophecy of the Savior," you could respond as you open your Bible and show the querist the prophecies from the Old Testament and their corresponding fulfillments in the New Testament. "Why do you have the hope of living with God in heaven in eternity?" still another asks. "Because God, who cannot lie, made the promise to those who follow Him faithfully," you might reply. (Titus 1:2). Your study of God's Word will prepare you to answer and, in the process, will make you personally stronger in the faith and better prepared to face Satan's attacks.

When we are ready and prepared to defend our hope, not only do we personally benefit, but those to whom we give our defense benefit. Have you ever looked at I Peter 3:15 as an evangelistic passage? It pictures an opportunity not just to defend our hope, but also to tell the non-believer of our hope. Some who will ask us of our hope will be doing so for the purpose of ridiculing us. On the other hand, some who ask us will be doing so because they genuinely want to know. They see something different in us that they haven't been able to find. They see the hope that they don't have and they want to know how we attained it. What a grand opportunity to teach the Gospel!

The end of I Peter 3:15 as well as verse 16 support the thought that this passage can also be viewed as evangelistic in nature. Verse 15 closes with an emphasis on the proper attitude that we must have when we give a defense for our hope. We must give our defense with meekness and fear.

To speak with meekness means to do so with a kind and gentle disposition. We are trying to win a soul when we teach God's Word to someone. Even if we are being challenged and being spoken to disrespectfully, we are still trying to win a soul. Paul said to speak the truth in love (Ephesians 4:15). Becoming defensive, showing impatience, yelling, or responding to those who question our hope in any other type of irritable manner will not be conducive to a productive study of the Bible. Granted, it can be very difficult to remain calm when someone asks us about our hope in an aggressive, attacking way. In these situations, we would do well to think of how Jesus answered those who questioned Him. His focus was to seek and to save the lost (Luke 19:10). In all of His interactions with other people, He remained conscious of the fact that each individual was an eternal soul who needed salvation.

Besides giving our defense with meekness, we are to offer it with fear. It is an awesome responsibility to teach the Gospel. James wrote, "My brethren, let not many of you become teachers, knowing that we shall receive a stricter judgment." (James 3:1). He was not discouraging us from teaching. Such would have been a contradiction of the Great Commission (Matthew 28:18-20). Instead, James was saying that we should take the teaching of God's Word very seriously for we shall be held accountable for what we say. When someone asks us a reason for our hope, our words should be carefully chosen and supported with Scripture. We endanger both our own souls and the souls of those to whom we make our defense if we teach error.

Peter continued the thought of verse 15 in the next verse. "Having a good conscience, that when they defame you as evildoers, those who revile your good conduct in Christ may be ashamed." (I Peter 3:16).

As we continue to look at this passage from an evangelistic standpoint, we note here that the defense of our hope must be consistent with the lives that we live. In this context, it appears that the original readers were being questioned by those who were antagonistic toward God. They were looking for some evidence of hypocrisy in the lives of these Christians. It would have been easy to discredit the Gospel message if it did not mesh with the lives of those who were proclaiming it.

Jesus warned us about causing others to stumble through ungodly examples (Luke 17:1-2). Paul said, "*Let* love *be* without hypocrisy. Abhor what is evil. Cling to what is good." (Romans 12:9). As Christians, we are being observed by the world. People want to see if we are who we say we are. If we claim on one hand to be followers of God and His Word while on the other hand we live worldly lives, we will effectively close the ears of those we want to lead to Christ. Paul asked, "You, therefore, who teach another, do you not teach yourself?" (Romans 2:21). As one individual noted in regard to a life that is inconsistent with one's words, "What you do speaks so loudly that I cannot hear what you say."

The defense of our hope is to be firmly founded in God's Word. Our lives must be as well. The balance of Peter's words in I Peter 3:16 bring Daniel to mind. The mighty prophet had been exalted to a high position in the service of king Darius. His peers had determined to find something bad in him so that they might accuse him of wrongdoing and get him removed from his position. Daniel 6:4 says, "So the governors and satraps sought to find *some* charge against Daniel concerning the kingdom; but they could find no charge or fault, because he *was* faithful; nor was there any error or fault found in him." The life of purity lived by Daniel is the same one urged by Peter. Live in such a manner that when others make a charge of evil against you, no one will believe it.

Do we have hope in our hearts? If so, are we prepared and ready to make a defense of it? If we are prepared and ready, will we make the defense in meekness and fear? Are we living in such a way that people will see that we are honoring the God who gives us the hope that we have?

It is a precious privilege to be able to tell the world about our Lord. Jesus expects us to be an influence for good (Matthew 5:13-16). May each of us rise to the occasion when someone asks us to defend our hope. Preparing to give a defense benefits us spiritually. Taking action by actually giving that defense can lead lost souls to eternal salvation.

EXERCISE YOUR MIND

True or False

1. The original readers of I Peter had very easy lives as Christians.   T   F
2. The Greek word translated, "ready" in I Peter 3:15 can also be translated, "prepared."   T   F
3. Our defense of our hope begins with us sanctifying God in our hearts.   T   F
4. Daily study of the Bible is not important.
5. Feelings and opinions are suitable evidence for our hope.   T   F

Multiple Choice

1. When it comes to defending our spiritual hope, we should:
    A) not worry about it;
    B) always be prepared and ready;
    C) leave it up to the preacher to defend it for us.

2. Hosea said that Israel was destroyed:
    A) for a lack of knowledge;
    B) for knowing too much of God's Word;
    C) because God didn't care about them.

3. The religious division that exists today:
   A) is approved by God;
   B) is the result of no one being able to understand the Bible;
   C) leads to confusion.
4. Our feelings:
   A) can deceive us;
   B) are always right;
   C) should be our primary guide in spiritual matters.
5. When we prepare ourselves to defend our hope:
   A) we benefit from the study of God's Word;
   B) we waste our time;
   C) we will not benefit at all.

Fill in the Blanks

(Note: All scripture quotations are taken from the New King James Version and can be found in this lesson.)
1. "If then you were _____ with _____, seek those things which are _____, where Christ is, sitting at the right hand of _____. Set your _____ on things _____, not on things on the _____."
2. "Be _____ to present _____ approved to _____, a _____ who does not need to be _____, rightly _____ the word of _____."
3. "My _____, let not many of you become _____, knowing that we shall _____ a stricter _____."
4. "Having a good _____, that when they defame you as _____, those who _____ your good _____ in Christ may be _____."
5. "*Let* love *be* without _____. Abhor what is _____. Cling to what is _____."

Questions for Discussion

1. What are some ways in which our faith is tried or tested? _____
   _____
   _____
   _____

2. What do the words, "fiery trial" suggest about the intensity of the suffering that these early Christians were facing and were going to face? _____
   _____
   _____
   _____

3. Discuss the difference between being prepared and being ready as suggested by the word translated, "ready" in I Peter 3:15. _____
   _____
   _____
   _____

4. Why must we be both prepared AND ready to give a defense of the hope that is in us? _____
   _____
   _____
   _____

5. Why is knowledge of the Bible important for our spiritual growth?
   _____
   _____

In Defense of Hope

6. Why is knowledge of the Bible necessary in our efforts to defend our hope to those who ask us? _____

7. What should we do or say if we are talking to someone about the Bible and we are not able to answer one of their questions? _____

8. Does it seem to you that there is a lack of knowledge of God's Word in the world today? Explain your answer. _____

9. Does it seem to you that there is a lack of knowledge of God's Word in the church today? Explain your answer. _____

10. Why would a person place his or her opinions above the Word of God? _____

_____

_____

_____

11. Why would a person place his or her feelings above the Word of God?_____

_____

_____

_____

12. Give an example of how one would defend hope with an attitude of meekness. _____

_____

_____

_____

13. Give an example of how you would respond to someone who was angrily attacking your hope._____

_____

_____

_____

14. Why is hypocrisy in our lives so detrimental to our ability to defend our hope to others? _____

_____

_____

_____

15. Do you know any Christians whose lives are clearly consistent with the hope that they have in God? Tell what stands out about them that makes it evident that they have this hope. _____

_____

_____

_____

SEARCH THE SCRIPTURES

(Note: For this section, you will find a good concordance helpful. All scripture quotations are taken from the New King James Version.)

Where is the following Bible verse located? _____

"'The LORD *is* my portion,' says my soul, 'Therefore I hope in Him!'"

Chapter Six

Hope and Obedience

Memory Work:

"And everyone who has this hope in Him purifies himself, just as He is pure." (I John 3:3)

Hope is a producer. It produces joy in the midst of sadness, peace in the throes of distress, and calm in the heat of chaos.

Hope is also a motivator. When days are difficult and the outlook is bleak, hope is what gets us up in the morning and keeps us going. Many successful business people will tell you about the down times they had in growing their companies and how many times in their careers it was hope alone that made them push ahead.

Hope serves as a motivator in the spiritual realm as well. Because of our hope of heaven and because we know that heaven is only for those who do God's will (Matthew 7:21-23), we press on in faithful obedience to our Lord. Though Satan constantly challenges us, we refuse to succumb to his temptations to stop obeying God because of our hope of eternal rest at the end of our journey. Like Paul, we "press toward the goal for the prize of the upward call of God in Christ Jesus." (Philippians 3:14).

This chapter's memory verse shows the correlation between hope and obedience. The verse just before it states, "Beloved, now we are children of God; and it has not yet been revealed what we shall be, but we know that when He is revealed, we shall be like Him, for we shall see Him as He is." (I John 3:2). This is the ultimate hope of the Christian. We want to be with the Lord in heaven in eternity. Ideally, that is our burning desire. It is a desire that should be so ingrained in our hearts that we will not allow anything or anyone to remove it.

Just having the desire to go to heaven is not enough though. Given the choice between heaven and hell, those who claim to be Christians will always say that they want to go to heaven. Those who follow the gods of this world typically have a belief in some type of reward after this life is over. Even some who do not believe in Deity at all like the thought of a place of eternal peace. Most people want to have eternal rest and joy after they leave this world, but, according to Jesus, few actually choose the path that leads in that direction. The Savior said, "Enter by the narrow gate; for wide *is* the gate and broad *is* the way that leads to destruction, and there are many who go in by it. Because narrow *is* the gate and difficult *is* the way which leads to life, and there are few who find it." (Matthew 7:13-14). Just desiring heaven is not sufficient to get us there.

Heaven is a place of purity. Revelation 21:27 tells us, "But there shall by no means enter it anything that defiles, or causes an abomination or a lie, but only those who are written in the Lamb's Book of Life." Because it is a place of purity and because God Himself is holy, He requires us to be pure and holy in life if we want to be with Him in eternity. "But as He who called you *is* holy, you also be holy in all *your* conduct, because it is written, 'Be holy, for I am holy.'" (I Peter 1:15-16).

The word translated, "purifies" in I John 3:3 is in the present tense, active voice, and indicative mood in the Greek language. This means that it is continuous action. Everyone who has the hope of being with the Lord continues to purify himself or herself. It is not a one-time action. We continue to obey God and grow in Him because of our hope of being with Him.

How is it possible for us to purify ourselves? Isn't it the blood of Jesus that purifies us? Indeed it is the blood of Jesus that purifies us, but that purification comes with our obedience. Luke summed up Peter's

Pentecost sermon by saying, "And with many other words he testified and exhorted them, saying, 'Be saved from this perverse generation.'" (Acts 2:40). The King James Version reads, "Save yourselves from this untoward generation." Some have scoffed at this passage, saying that it suggests we can save ourselves. In Acts 22:16 we find Ananias telling Saul, "And now why are you waiting? Arise and be baptized, and wash away your sins, calling on the name of the Lord." Again, some minimize the impact of that verse because in their minds it is saying that we save ourselves. Both verses show the necessity of our response to the Gospel. Jesus saves through His blood (Acts 4:12), but, as we have already noted, not everyone is going to be saved. Salvation comes through obedience. The Lord places us into the body of Christ when we obey His Gospel (Galatians 3:27). In one sense, then, we do save or purify ourselves because there is no purification without the blood of Jesus and yet the only way we can enjoy the blessings of the blood of Jesus is through our obedience to His Word. This is not salvation by works that we have devised. Instead, it is simply adhering to the parameters that God has set for being redeemed.

These facts about purification apply even after we obey the Gospel and are cleansed of past sins. John wrote to Christians, "If we say that we have fellowship with Him, and walk in darkness, we lie and do not practice the truth. But if we walk in the light as He is in the light, we have fellowship with one another, and the blood of Jesus Christ His Son cleanses us from all sin." (I John 1:6-7). As Christians, we are purified with the blood of Jesus when we walk with Him in obedience.

How much do you want to see Jesus? To be sure, every eye shall see Him (Revelation 1:7) for all who have ever lived will be gathered before Him in judgment (Matthew 25:31-46). How much do you want to see Jesus and hear Him say to you, "Come, you blessed of My Father, inherit the kingdom prepared for you from the foundation of the world"? (Matthew 25:34). The Lord is pure. His eternal dwelling place is pure. We want to go there. We face Satan every day and battle him because of our hope of heaven. To be there, we ourselves must be pure, and to be pure, we must obey the pure and perfect will of God that has been revealed and that we can read in the Bible.

Another verse that references the relationship between hope and obedience is Hebrews 3:5-6. "And Moses indeed *was* faithful in all His house as a servant, for a testimony of those things which would be spoken *afterward*, but Christ as a Son over His own house, whose house we are if we hold fast the confidence and the rejoicing of the hope firm to the end." In this passage the writer has demonstrated a similarity as well as a difference between Moses and Jesus. The difference is that Moses was a servant but Christ is the Son. The similarity is that both Moses and the Christ were faithful. Moses was faithful in all his house. Christ was faithful (implied) in His own house. Christ's house is His church (I Timothy 3:15). We are that house if we have obeyed His Gospel.

The words, "hold fast" and "firm to the end" indicate a lifelong faithfulness. In between those words we read of "the rejoicing of the hope." In fact, the entire context of the third chapter of Hebrews and a good portion of the fourth chapter treat the subject of faithful diligence in obeying God. Hebrews 3:14 reads, "For we have become partakers of Christ if we hold the beginning of our confidence steadfast to the end."

Do you want to see the Lord's smiling face? Do you want to hear His wonderful words of welcome? Is the hope of that marvelous meeting deeply rooted in your heart? Don't let Satan steal it away by allowing him to convince you that his way is better than God's way. Cling with all of your might to the Lord and do not leave His way. Your hope will be rewarded in eternity.

Hebrews 6:11 is yet another verse that should be considered in this chapter's study. "And we desire that each one of you show the same diligence to the full assurance of hope until the end." Keeping in mind that much of the focus of the letter to the Hebrew Christians was to encourage them to remain faithful, we're not surprised that the writer so quickly revisits the subject of hope and obedience after having addressed it just three chapters earlier. In Hebrews 6:10 we read about their work and labor of love. In Hebrews 6:12 we find the exhortation to not be sluggish but to instead imitate those who inherit God's promise through faith and patience. The necessity of obedience in order to be with God in heaven is clearly seen in these verses.

Sandwiched in between the comments about faithfulness is the writer's reference to "the full assurance of hope." The phrase indicates that Christians should be diligent in their faithfulness to God with regard to or with a view toward the full assurance of hope. We should obey God because of our confident hope of the reward that He will give the faithful in heaven. As Christians, we should build our hope to such a pinnacle of certainty that we will not be swayed by anything that tempts us away or by anyone who tries to lead us anywhere but toward eternal life with God. The more our assurance of hope grows, the more committed we become to obeying God. The more diligently we search God's Word to learn and to live His will, the more assured we become in our hope.

Do you have the hope of heaven? When you look around you at the sin and suffering in the world, do you look forward to going to be with the Lord? When you yourself struggle with temptation and the trials of life, do you look up in hope with the full assurance that God will bless you as He has promised to bless all those who follow Him faithfully up to the moment of death? Don't give up on that hope now. Keep walking with God. Keep going and growing in Him. If you do, you will see Him in all His glory. You will rest from your labors (Revelation 14:13). Keep the hope burning bright by walking with the Lord in loving obedience to Him.

God's promises are tremendous. They are the basis of our hope. We must never forget, however, that many of God's promises, including that of eternal life, are conditional. This is a vital truth that is often overlooked or even dismissed by those who choose to believe either that we don't need to do anything to be saved or that once we are saved we are always saved.

Returning to the letter to the Hebrews, we read in chapter four, verse one, "Therefore, since a promise remains of entering His rest, let us fear lest any of you seem to have come short of it." As was noted earlier, the context of chapter three and much of chapter four centers around encouraging faithfulness. Here the writer had just referenced Israel's wandering in the wilderness and the fact that many of those who had been delivered from Egyptian bondage never got to see the earthly promised land of Canaan. The thirteenth and fourteenth chapters of Numbers tell us why. The people had turned away from God out of fear and actually wanted to go back to captivity. Hebrews 3:19 refers to this as unbelief and indicates that that was the reason they were not allowed to enter Canaan.

With that example in mind, chapter four of Hebrews opens with a dire warning. "Don't be like Israel in the wilderness." We are not looking for physical Canaan as a reward today. We have our eyes on spiritual Canaan. God promised physical Israel that they could enter the land of Canaan. Why did some of them not go in? It was because of their disobedience.

God has promised heaven to spiritual Israel (Christians). Why will some not go in? It will be because of disobedience. Hebrews 4:11 exhorts, "Let us therefore be diligent to enter that rest, lest anyone fall according to the same example of disobedience."

The hope that we are blessed to enjoy as Christians did not come at a cheap price. It was purchased with the blood of Jesus. Paul wrote that giving our lives to and for the one who gave His all for us is reasonable or logical. "I beseech you therefore, brethren, by the mercies of God, that you present your bodies a living sacrifice, holy, acceptable to God, *which is* your reasonable service. And do not be conformed to this world, but be transformed by the renewing of your mind, that you may prove what *is* that good and acceptable and perfect will of God." (Romans 12:1-2). Since the Lord gave His very best, thus giving us a reason for the hope of heaven, should we not in return give Him our very best in loving, faithful obedience?

EXERCISE YOUR MIND

True or False

1. Hope can motivate us to greater obedience to God.   T   F
2. Everyone who desires to go to heaven will go.   T   F
3. We should live lives of purity because the Lord is pure.   T   F
4. Even after we become Christians, we should strive to live lives of purity.
5. God wants us to be faithful to Him unto death.   T   F

Multiple Choice

1. Hope:
   A) motivates us to obey God;
   B) has little impact on our spiritual lives;
   C) is nothing more than a mere wish.

2. We seek purity in our lives because:
   A) everyone else is seeking it;
   B) Satan wants us to be pure;
   C) our Lord is pure.

3. The writer of Hebrews wrote of:
   A) the possibility of hope;
   B) the uncertainty of hope;
   C) the full assurance of hope.

4. God's promise of salvation is:
   A) conditional;

B) guaranteed for everyone, no matter what type of lives they live;
C) available to no one.
5. A Christian:
A) can never fall away from God and lose his or her soul;
B) never sins;
C) can sin and lose his or her soul if they do not repent.

Fill in the Blanks

(Note: All scripture quotations are taken from the New King James Version and can be found in this lesson.)

1. "_____, now we are _____ of God; and it has not yet been _____ what we shall be, but we know that when He is _____, we shall be _____ Him, for we shall see Him as He is."
2. "Enter by the _____ gate; for _____ *is* the gate and _____ *is* the way that leads to _____, and there are _____ who go in by it. Because _____ *is* the gate and _____ *is* the way which leads to _____, and there are _____ who find it."
3. "But as He who called you *is* _____, you also be _____ in all *your* _____, because it is written, 'Be _____, for I am _____.'"
4. "And now why are you _____? _____ and be _____, and wash away your _____, calling on the _____ of the _____."
5. "I _____ you therefore, brethren, by the _____ of God, that you present your _____ a living _____, holy, acceptable to God, *which is* your _____ service. And do not be _____ to this world, but be _____ by the _____ of your mind, that you may _____ what *is* that _____ and _____ and perfect _____ of God."

Questions for Discussion

1. This chapter opens by noting that hope produces and motivates. What else can you think of that hope does for us? _____

2. What did Paul mean when he said that he pressed toward the goal? What can we learn from this? _____

3. Why do some people choose not to obey God? _____

4. Why is the way to eternal destruction called wide and broad?

5. Why is the way to eternal life called narrow and difficult?

6. Name some ways in which we can demonstrate holiness in our lives? _____
_____
_____
_____

7. Is it important for those around us to see us living in a holy manner? Explain your answer. _____
_____
_____
_____

8. What can we do to continually purify ourselves? _____
_____
_____
_____

9. When we teach that one must obey God in order to be saved, are we teaching salvation by works? Explain your answer. _____
_____
_____
_____

10. Must we continue to obey God even after we become Christians? Why or why not? _____
_____
_____
_____

Hope and Obedience 69

11. Cite an example of how Jesus obeyed the Father. _____

    _____

    _____

12. What do the words, "hold fast" and "firm to the end" indicate in regard to our faithfulness? _____

    _____

    _____

13. What does it mean to have "the full assurance of hope"? _____

    _____

    _____

14. Besides the promise of salvation, name at least one other promise of God that is conditional. _____

    _____

    _____

15. Discuss the difference between being conformed to this world and being transformed by the renewing of your mind. _____

    _____

    _____

SEARCH THE SCRIPTURES

(Note: For this section, you will find a good concordance helpful. All scripture quotations are taken from the New King James Version.)

Where is the following Bible verse located? _____

"LORD, I hope for Your salvation, and I do Your commandments."

CHAPTER SEVEN

Hope for Today

Memory Work:

"Be of good courage, and He shall strengthen your heart, all you who hope in the LORD." (Psalm 31:24)

Thus far we have primarily examined hope as it pertains to its fulfillment in eternity. Heaven is the ultimate hope of every faithful Christian. Along our path toward eternal life, however, are several mile markers of hope that lift us up and help us deal with the day to day challenges we face in this world. We don't have to wait until heaven to experience all of the blessings of hope. The Lord rewards our hope time and time again even here on earth.

Romans 3:23 says, "for all have sinned and fall short of the glory of God." Even as Christians, we often fail miserably. We come up short of God's glory time and time again. Why do we keep going? It's because of our hope in God's promise that He will forgive us when we turn back to Him with penitent hearts (I John 1:7-9).

Think for a moment about some of the great people of faith who failed God. David committed adultery with Bathsheba and then was an accomplice in the death of her husband, Uriah (II Samuel 11). When he acknowledged his sins, he turned to God in humble confession and repentance (Psalm 51). While he expressed his anguish over his transgressions in that Psalm, he also expressed his hope in God's compassion. Psalm 51:17 reads, "The sacrifices of God *are* a broken spirit, a broken and a contrite heart - these, O God, You will not despise." David had hope that, even though he had sinned against God, he would find mercy as he humbled himself before the Lord.

Peter is another example of one who failed the Lord. He had boldly declared His allegiance to Jesus not just once, but twice, when Jesus told him and the other apostles that He was going to be killed and that they were going to run away from Him. "Peter answered and said to Him, 'Even if all are made to stumble because of You, I will never be made to stumble.'" (Matthew 26:33). "Peter said to Him, 'Even if I have to die with You, I will not deny You!'" (Matthew 26:35). Sadly, he did crumble under the pressure of the moment when pressed to admit that he was one of Jesus' disciples. He not only denied Jesus, but angrily cursed that he did not know the man (Matthew 26:74). Matthew 26:75 says that he went out and wept bitterly following the denial, an act that demonstrated a heart that had been broken by sin. It was, of course, this same Peter who stood in the midst of thousands on the day of Pentecost following Jesus' ascension to heaven and boldly proclaimed the Gospel (Acts 2). It was this same Peter who was arrested and beaten for preaching the Gospel (Acts 4:3; 5:40). It was this same Peter who would eventually give his life for the Lord (John 21:18-19; II Peter 1:14). Rather than allowing his failure to destroy him, Peter allowed the hope that he had in God to propel him to accomplish amazing tasks in the Lord's service. He did not give up.

The apostle Paul is yet another example of one who had failed God. As a Jew, Paul (then known as Saul) had fought against the Lord (Acts 9:4-5). After he obeyed the Gospel, he often spoke of his gratitude for God's mercy. He told the Corinthian church, "But by the grace of God I am what I am." (I Corinthians 15:10). He wrote to Timothy of how he had been a blasphemer, a persecutor, and an insolent man and yet had found grace with God (I Timothy 1:12-16). Yet, even though he had been delivered from past sins, Paul said that he still frequently came short of God's standards (Romans 7:15-23). He cried out, "O wretched man that I am! Who will deliver me from this body of death?" (Romans 7:24). Though grieved by his sins, Paul's hope in God's mercy was clearly expressed in the next phrase, "I thank God through Jesus Christ our Lord." (Romans 7:25). He kept going because of the hope he had in God's forgiveness.

Again, we as Christians often fail miserably. Sin breaks our hearts. Were it not for the hope that we have of God's forgiveness, sin would also break our spirits. Because of our hope that, "if we confess our sins, He is faithful and just to forgive us *our* sins and to cleanse us from all unrighteousness," (I John 1:9), we press on, hopefully learning from our transgressions and being better prepared for Satan's next attack.

Even when we fail God, there is hope if we will repent. In like manner, even when we face the most difficult of life's challenges, there is hope.

The hope in Jeremiah's words in the third chapter of Lamentations is astounding. The first 19 verses of that chapter recount the troubles that Israel had been suffering. Any one of these would have been enough to bring down and keep down the strongest person, yet, in Lamentations 3:21, the writer spoke of hope. The reason for this hope was expressed in the verses that follow.

> "*Through* the Lord's mercies we are not consumed, Because His compassions fail not. *They are* new every morning; great *is* Your faithfulness. 'The Lord *is* my portion,' says my soul, 'Therefore I hope in Him!' The Lord *is* good to those who wait for Him, to the soul *who* seeks Him. *It is* good that *one* should hope and wait quietly for the salvation of the Lord." (Lamentations 3:22-26).

While Israel's difficulties were brought about by their sins, and sometimes ours are as well, we know that often challenges come into our lives through no fault of our own. We might develop an illness, get dismissed from a job because the company goes out of business, be hurt by the sins of others, or experience hardships through a multitude of other means. Why do we keep going? It's because of our hope in the

God-given mercies of each new day. Even if the new day brings with it greater distresses than the one before, we still know three facts. First, we know that with every tick of the clock we are getting closer to our eternal home. "And *do* this, knowing the time, that now *it is* high time to awake out of sleep; for now our salvation *is* nearer than when we *first* believed." (Romans 13:11). Second, as Paul said, the afflictions of this life are only momentary when compared to eternity (II Corinthians 4:17). Third, each of life's challenges is an opportunity for us to glorify God. When Paul was told that his thorn in the flesh would not be removed and that the Lord's grace was sufficient for him in his suffering, he wrote, "Therefore I take pleasure in infirmities, in reproaches, in needs, in persecutions, in distresses, for Christ's sake. For when I am weak, then I am strong." (II Corinthians 12:10). These precious thoughts, each of which is couched in God's Word, are rewards for our hope.

We could go on for several pages discussing the earthly blessings of hope, but for the sake of time just two more will be mentioned here. As stated in this chapter's memory verse, those who hope in the Lord can take courage because God will strengthen our hearts.

Satan would have us believe that he is stronger than God. We look around and see how wicked our society has become. We often find ourselves in the minority when it comes to standing for what is right. Being mistreated for our faith causes us to become discouraged. Continued abuse could cause us to give up hope. How many times have we thought to ourselves, "No one really wants to hear the Gospel anymore"? That type of thinking is exactly what Satan wants because he knows that it will cause us to stop spreading God's Word and perhaps even stop obeying it ourselves.

According to Psalm 31:24, hope produces strength and strength engenders courage. What's more, it develops these blessings in our hearts, the very core of our being. It is strength and courage that allows us to boldly speak and live God's Word, despite the number of detractors who would seek to stop us. We gain the strength and courage we need as we cling to the hope that we have in God.

Hope is alive today in the hearts of faithful Christians. We can see it, we can feel it, we can know it on a daily basis. It is alive because the Lord, the author of hope, is Himself alive and He will never depart from us. "I will never leave you nor forsake you." (Hebrews 13:5). "For I am persuaded that neither death nor life, nor angels nor principalities nor powers, nor things present nor things to come, nor height nor depth, nor any other created thing, shall be able to separate us from the love of God which is in Christ Jesus our Lord." (Romans 8:38-39).

Hope is alive today because our God is faithful to us. "God *is* faithful, by whom you were called into the fellowship of His Son, Jesus Christ our Lord." (I Corinthians 1:9). "No temptation has overtaken you except such as is common to man; but God *is* faithful, who will not allow you to be tempted beyond what you are able, but with the temptation will also make the way of escape, that you may be able to bear *it*." (I Corinthians 10:13). "Now may the God of peace Himself sanctify you completely; and may your whole spirit, soul, and body be preserved blameless at the coming of our Lord Jesus Christ. He who calls you *is* faithful, who also will do *it*." (I Thessalonians 5:23-24).

Hope is alive today because we serve the God of second chances. "The Lord is not slack concerning *His* promise, as some count slackness, but is longsuffering toward us, not willing that any should perish but that all should come to repentance." (II Peter 3:9). He is aware of our sins and yet He still wants to save us.

Hope is alive today because our God is the God of deliverance. Shadrach, Meshach, and Abednego were commanded by king Nebuchadnezzar to fall down and worship the idol he had created. When they refused, the king said to them, "Now if you are ready at the time you hear the sound of the horn, flute, harp, lyre, *and* psaltery, in symphony with all kinds of music, and you fall down and worship the image which I have made, *good!* But if you do not worship, you shall be cast immediately into the midst of a burning fiery furnace. And who *is* the god who will deliver you from my hands?" (Daniel 3:15). The three faithful men replied, "If that *is the case,* our God whom we serve is able to deliver us from the burning fiery furnace, and He will deliver *us* from your hand, O king." (Daniel 3:17). The verses that follow demonstrate that God did indeed deliver them. When king Darius came to the mouth of the lions' den to ask Daniel if God had been able to deliver him from those ferocious beasts, he heard Daniel reply, "My God sent His angel and shut the lions' mouths, so that they have not hurt me, because I was found innocent before Him; and also, O king, I have done no wrong before you." (Daniel 6:22). As we sometimes sing, "Our God is able to deliver thee!"

Hope is alive today because the Divinely inspired Word that produces our hope is alive. "For the word of God *is* living and powerful, and sharper than any two-edged sword, piercing even to the division of soul and spirit, and of joints and marrow, and is a discerner of the thoughts and intents of the heart." (Hebrews 4:12).

We have constant reminders of God's presence and care. They show themselves in the forms of our physical blessings, our friends, our families, the church, the beauty of nature and more. When we start to feel down and lose hope, we can go to God's Word and be strengthened in our hope, but we can also look around us to see evidence of God's existence and of His love for us.

The joy that we know as Christians is a blessing of hope. The peace that we know as Christians is a blessing of hope. A positive outlook on life is a blessing of hope. We can partake of these blessings each and every day.

We hope for heaven. If we are faithful unto death, one day we will enjoy a full realization of that hope. In the meantime, we can see hope's blessings all around us. We just have to open our eyes. John wrote, "You are of God, little children, and have overcome them, because He who is in you is greater than he who is in the world." (I John 4:4). As challenging as this life might sometimes become, the blessings of God are still all around us. God will always be superior to Satan. Through Him we can gain the ultimate victory in eternity (I Corinthians 15:57), but also we can enjoy the blessings of our hope on a daily basis, blessings that spur us on and remind us that God is always near and that we should never give up.

EXERCISE YOUR MIND

True or False

1. We can enjoy the blessings of hope in this life. T F
2. God does not want us to be saved. T F
3. The afflictions of this life are only temporary. T F
4. The Lord is difficult to find when we are in trouble. T F
5. The blessings of hope are all around us. T F

Multiple Choice

1. As Christians, we:
    A) never sin;
    B) often fail miserably;
    C) are perfect.

2. After Peter denied Jesus, he:
    A) wept bitterly;
    B) did not think he had done anything wrong;
    C) was happy.

3. Paul knew that he could only be delivered from his sins by:
    A) the law of Moses;
    B) Jesus Christ;
    C) his feelings.

4. God's compassions:
    A) fail not;
    B) are new every morning;
    C) both A and B.

5. Hope:
    A) was only for those who lived in the first century;

B) is not attainable;
C) is alive today.

Fill in the Blanks

(Note: All scripture quotations are taken from the New King James Version and can be found in this lesson.)
1. "For all have _____ and _____ _____ of the _____ of God."
2. "And *do* this, knowing the _____, that now *it is* high time to _____ out of _____; for now our _____ *is* nearer than when we *first* _____."
3. "Therefore I take _____ in _____, in _____, in _____, in _____, in _____, for Christ's sake. For when I am _____, then I am _____."
4. "God *is* _____, by whom you were called into the _____ of His Son, Jesus Christ our _____."
5. "You are of _____, little children, and have _____ them, because He who is in you is _____ than he who is in the _____."

Questions for Discussion

1. What are some other blessings of hope that we experience in this life? _____

   _____

   _____

   _____

2. Why do we sometimes fail God? _____

   _____

3. What can we do to help us not fail Him so often?

4. Why does God forgive us when we turn to Him in humble and penitent obedience?

5. How often will God forgive us when we turn to Him in humble and penitent obedience?

6. What did Paul mean when he referred to himself as the chief of sinners (I Timothy 1:15)?

7. How can knowing that we are getting closer to eternity each second inspire hope within us?

8. Even though life's challenges are only temporary when compared to eternity, do they seem that way when we are in the midst of dealing with them? Why or why not? _____

9. What blessings could come out of the difficulties we face?

10. What did Paul mean when he wrote, "For when I am weak, then I am strong"? _____

11. How does Satan try to make us believe that he is stronger than God? _____

12. How do we know that God is stronger than Satan? _____

Hope for Today

13. How does knowing that God is faithful build hope within us?

14. What are some things from which God delivers us and how does He do it?

15. What are some other daily reminders of God's presence and care for us?

SEARCH THE SCRIPTURES

(Note: For this section, you will find a good concordance helpful. All scripture quotations are taken from the New King James Version.)

Where is the following Bible verse located? _____

"But for him who is joined to all the living there is hope, for a living dog is better than a dead lion."

Chapter Eight

Hope in the Psalms

Memory Work:

"Happy *is he* who *has* the God of Jacob for his help, whose hope *is* in the Lord his God." (Psalm 146:5)

Although hope is found throughout the Bible, there are three books in particular that stand out when it comes to a treatment of the subject. They are Psalms, Jeremiah, and Romans. In this chapter and the two to follow, we will consider what these inspired writers had to say about hope.

The book of Psalms encompasses so many aspects of our lives. Therein we learn of our creation at the hand of God (Psalm 8), our ability to fall into sin (Psalm 51), our need for God's redemption (Psalm 86), and the power of God's Word to guide us to His deliverance (Psalm 119). From birth (Psalm 139) to death (Psalm 23) and every moment between, the Psalms indeed constitute "a lamp to my feet and a light to my path." (Psalm 119:105).

Although the entire book of Psalms covers a wide range of topics, it seems that we most often find ourselves turning to it when we feel the need to be lifted up. Each of us likely has a favorite Psalm that soothes us when we are troubled. Many Christians can quote Psalm 23 and perhaps do so quite often. The Psalms are an oft visited refuge of comfort and strength. They bring our souls the peace and joy we so often crave. They also inspire hope within us.

This chapter will consider verses in the Psalms that use the word, "hope." Obviously we won't be able to treat every Psalm, but perhaps a selection will urge us all to search the Psalms more diligently for the words of hope that are found in so many of them.

Beginning with the memory verse above, we find that hope brings happiness. More specifically, hope in God brings happiness. Even more specifically than that, this happiness comes from hoping in Jehovah God, the God of Jacob.

There are many "gods" that have been created by mankind. Jeremiah wrote, "For *according to* the number of your cities were your gods, O Judah; and *according to* the number of the streets of Jerusalem you have set up altars to *that* shameful thing, altars to burn incense to Baal." (Jeremiah 11:13). This was written to one nation at a particular point in time. How many different "gods" were worshipped prior to this, not only by Judah, but by the other nations of the world? How many have been created and worshipped since? Were we able to count them all, we might find that the number of "gods" throughout time is in the millions.

Knowing that some had turned and would turn to man-made "gods," the Psalmist's words were carefully chosen by the Holy Spirit to isolate the one true God as the source of happiness. Hope in worldly "gods" is fruitless and leads to destruction rather than happiness because those "gods" are the products of man's imagination. As has already been stated in this book, for hope to be real, it has to be firmly grounded. Hope in a "god" rather than Jehovah God is baseless because that "god" doesn't exist.

Jehovah God, the one true God who was worshipped by Jacob, is God alone. He told Judah, "I, *even* I, *am* the LORD, and besides Me *there is* no savior." (Isaiah 43:11). He quickly repeated that truth five more times to impress upon Judah that there was (and is) no God other than Him (Isaiah 44:6,8; 45:5,6,21). Those who hope in the one true God enjoy happiness and blessings because their hope is properly directed. Our God is pleased when we place our hope in Him. "The LORD takes pleasure in those who fear Him, in those who hope in His mercy." (Psalm 147:11).

Not only do the Psalms show us that hope in God brings happiness, they remind us that God is watching over and caring for those who hope in Him. Psalm 33:18 reads, "Behold, the eye of the LORD *is* on those who fear Him, on those who hope in His mercy." In a broad sense, God sees all. "The eyes of the LORD *are* in every place, keeping watch on the evil and the good." (Proverbs 15:3). Psalm 34:15 points out that God gives special attention to those who follow Him. "The eyes of the LORD *are* on the righteous, and His ears *are open* to their cry." The thought of God seeing our every move is intimidating to those who do not choose to follow Him. To those who choose to fear Him and live righteously, this thought brings comfort and joy. We can have hope because God sees our service (Hebrews 6:10). He is aware of our diligent effort to obey Him. He sees our struggles and He is there to help (Psalm 46:5).

The Psalms portray hope as something that helps us stand against the enemies of the righteous. In Psalm 38, the Psalmist wrote of how he had felt forsaken by those around him. His loved ones, friends and family had distanced themselves from him (Psalm 38:11). His enemies were trying to trap him (Psalm 38:12). In spite of this, his ears were closed to their taunts. The reason for this is seen in Psalm 38:15. "For in You, O LORD, I hope; You will hear, O Lord my God." With this hope in his heart, in spite of the abandonment and persecution of men, the Psalmist proceeded to beg the Lord to hear him and to help. He knew that he would continue to face rejection from mankind for his dedication to God, but he trusted that the God in whom He placed his trust and hope would heed his cries for aid.

Psalm 71 echoes the sentiment expressed in Psalm 38. This Psalm opens, "In You, O LORD, I put my trust; let me never be put to shame." (Psalm 71:1). The word translated, "trust" can also mean "hope" and is so rendered in Proverbs 14:32 in the King James Version. The writer declared, "For You are my hope, O Lord GOD; *You are* my trust from my youth." (Psalm 71:5). He then went on to talk about the evil attacks that were being hurled at him. Some were even going so far as to say, "'God has forsaken him; pursue and take him, for *there is* none to deliver *him.*'" (Psalm 71:11). Having already twice expressed his hope in God, he did so again in verse 14. "But I will hope continually, and will praise You yet more and more."

Those who despise righteousness will attack those who live in a Godly way (II Timothy 3:12). Sadly, those individuals have no hope. The hope that we have in God, however, can sustain us, even when it seems as though the world has turned against us.

The Psalms bring out the relationship between hope and patience. Patience is a very difficult virtue to develop because it is often, if not exclusively, developed through hardships. James wrote that "the testing of your faith produces patience." (James 1:3). He cited Job as an example of patience (James 5:11), and we are all well aware of the many ordeals in Job's life.

There are many reasons why we must learn patience. One is so that we learn how to trust God. Another is so we will remember that our greatest reward is in heaven. Lack of trust has caused people to worry, fear, and give up on God. Forgetting that our greatest reward is in heaven has caused some to forsake the Lord by falling in love with earth's pleasures. John said that we cannot love both the things of this world and God (I John 2:15).

Psalm 62:5 reads, "My soul, wait silently for God alone, for my expectation *is* from Him." The word translated, "expectation" is most commonly translated, "hope." This Psalm actually begins with the same exhortation to be patient. The balance of it contrasts the greatness and stability of God with the lowliness and emptiness of worldliness. We should wait on God because of His greatness. "He only *is* my rock and my salvation; *He is* my defense; I shall not be moved. In God *is* my salvation and my glory; the rock of my strength, *and* my refuge, *is* in God." (Psalm 62:6-7). While we are waiting patiently, we need not worry or wonder, fret or fume. Hope's role is to feed our patience. We hold out hope that God will care for us and provide what we need in His time.

Another Psalm that ties hope and patience together is Psalm 130. The Psalmist wrote, "I wait for the LORD, my soul waits, and in His word I do hope. My soul *waits* for the Lord more than those who watch for the morning - *yes, more than* those who watch for the morning." (Psalm 130:5-6). The next verse declares that there is mercy and abundant redemption with God. God will bless the faithful. We should not try to get ahead of Him but should instead trust His will, patiently wait for Him to give what is best, and cling tenaciously to our hope in Him each step of the way.

In Psalm 16 we find peace associated with hope. "I have set the LORD always before me; because *He is* at my right hand I shall not be moved. Therefore my heart is glad, and my glory rejoices; my flesh also will rest in hope." (Psalm 16:8-9). The word, "rest" suggests being settled or calm. We can be at peace internally because of our hope in God. That hope is promoted in us because the One in whom we hope is always before us.

It's ironic that, although so many people talk about peace and claim to want it, they don't realize how easy it is to find. It's not to be found in the words of mere men. It won't be discovered in a liquor bottle or an illicit drug. True peace is found only in the Lord. As Paul said, "Be anxious for nothing, but in everything by prayer and supplication, with thanksgiving, let your requests be made known to God; and the peace of God, which surpasses all understanding, will guard your hearts and minds through Christ Jesus." (Philippians 4:6-7). As we ponder God's promises, we build our hope and as we build our hope, we become more peaceful in our hearts.

Psalm 119 is typically referred to as a Torah psalm because of the many times it exalts God's Word. We have already stated in this book that we learn of and develop hope through God's Word. This Psalm frequently brings these two together.

"And take not the word of truth utterly out of my mouth, for I have hoped in Your ordinances." (Psalm 119:43). In verse 44 the Psalmist spoke of his determination to continually keep God's law. Thus we see that hope encourages obedience.

"Remember the word to Your servant, upon which You have caused me to hope." (Psalm 119:49). God's Word produces hope in those who believe it.

"Those who fear You will be glad when they see me, Because I have hoped in Your word." (Psalm 119:74). The hope we gain from God's Word can be an influence for good on others.

"My soul faints for Your salvation, but I hope in Your word." (Psalm 119:81). Hope that is couched in God's Word lifts us up.

"You *are* my hiding place and my shield; I hope in Your word." (Psalm 119:114). Through God's Word, we learn that God is our refuge and protector. This helps us have hope as we face life's challenges and Satan's temptations.

"I rise before the dawning of the morning, and cry for help; I hope in Your word." (Psalm 119:147). God has promised to daily bless those who follow Him faithfully (Matthew 6:33; cf. Psalm 37:25). This truth from His Word brings us hope as we begin each day.

We turn to the Psalms and we find many verses that speak of hope. Even those that don't actually use the word are often valuable sources for building hope. God's Word is a limitless wealth of spiritual treasure. The next time you sit down to read the book of Psalms, look specifically for passages that cause you to have greater hope. Write them down. Commit them to memory. Put them to good use for hardly a day goes by that we all don't need our hope to be lifted.

As I write these words I'm looking at a family treasure. It's a bookmark from my grandfather Gifford's Bible. Its fabric edges are frayed. It's once glistening gold words are now practically indistinguishable against the faded purple background. Under intense light, some of the words can be seen, but I don't need to see them for their memory is indelibly etched upon my heart. It's a bookmark from a funeral home received long, long ago. From top to bottom it is filled with lines that begin with, "If you need." Each line closes with a reference to a Bible passage. There are so many references to verses from Psalms on this eight inch by two inch place holder that one could know greater hope just by reading them alone. How thoughtful it was for the owners of that funeral home to provide these for grieving families.

This chapter closes with words from the psalm that is my personal favorite. Psalm 46:10 reads, "Be still, and know that I *am* God; I will be exalted among the nations, I will be exalted in the earth!" The words, "be still," serve as a reminder to settle down and relax. God is in control. We get so caught up in day to day affairs that we don't take time to just sit down and meditate upon the greatness of our God. We need to stop scurrying about in our minds and make time each day to think about who God is, how He blesses us, and how He has made it possible for us to be with Him in heaven. Settle down and concentrate on God. Open His Word and learn who He is. Look around and see what He has done and is doing. Dream about what He has in store in eternity for the faithful. Oh, what hope this will bring to your heart! "The Lord of hosts *is* with us; the God of Jacob *is* our refuge." (Psalm 46:11).

EXERCISE YOUR MIND

True or False

1. We often turn to Psalms when we feel the need to be lifted up. T F
2. There are many gods who can give us hope. T F
3. God is not concerned about His human creation. T F
4. Hope feeds patience. T F
5. Hope and peace have a close relationship to each other. T F

Multiple Choice

1. Mankind has created:
   A) no "gods";
   B) an untold number of "gods";
   C) only a few "gods."

2. Jehovah God said:
   A) He is the only God;
   B) He doesn't mind us worshipping manmade "gods";
   C) He is aware of at least one other God who is equal to Him.

3. God:
   A) sees all;
   B) is limited in His ability to see what we do;
   C) sees nothing that we do.

4. We can have hope because:
   A) Satan is not trying very hard to tempt us;
   B) no one is bothering those who are faithfully following God;
   C) God hears His faithful ones and He will deliver.

5. True peace:
   A) cannot be found;
   B) is found only in God through Jesus Christ;
   C) can be found by following the ways of the world.

Fill in the Blanks

(Note: All scripture quotations are taken from the New King James Version and can be found in this lesson.)

1. "I, *even* I, *am* the _____, and besides _____ *there is* no _____."

2. "Behold, the _____ of the _____ *is* on those who _____ Him, on those who _____ in His _____."

Hope in the Psalms

3. "For You are my _____, O Lord GOD; *You are* my _____ from my _____."
4. "My _____, wait _____ for God alone, for my _____ *is* from _____."
5. "You *are* my _____ place and my _____; I hope in Your _____."

Questions for Discussion

1. What other psalms give you hope? _____

2. What is your favorite psalm? Why is it your favorite? _____

3. Why do men and women create their own "gods"? _____

4. How do we know that Jehovah God is the one true God? _____

5. How does knowing God is watching bring hope and comfort?

6. Discuss Hebrews 6:10. How do these words give hope? _____

7. Why do some people not like those who are trying to follow God faithfully? _____

8. How are we to respond to those who do not like our commitment to follow God faithfully? _____

9. Discuss Psalm 71:14. What does it mean to hope continually?

10. What are some ways in which we can develop patience? _____

11. Why is patience so important to living the Christian life? _____

12. What are some reasons why we lose patience? _____

13. What lessons can we learn while we are "waiting" on God? _____

14. Why do we desire inner peace? _____

15. In what way or ways does hope encourage obedience? _____

SEARCH THE SCRIPTURES

(Note: For this section, you will find a good concordance helpful. All scripture quotations are taken from the New King James Version.)

Where is the following Bible verse located? _____

"I will say of the Lord, '*He is* my refuge and my fortress; my God, in Him I will trust.'"

Chapter Nine

Hope in Jeremiah

Memory Work:

"For I know the thoughts that I think toward you, says the Lord, thoughts of peace and not of evil, to give you a future and a hope." (Jeremiah 29:11)

It might be difficult to imagine the book of Jeremiah as a book that contains thoughts of hope. After all, its author is the one who has been nicknamed, "The Weeping Prophet." He wrote, "Oh, that my head were waters, and my eyes a fountain of tears, that I might weep day and night for the slain of the daughter of my people!" (Jeremiah 9:1). In addition to this and several other sorrowful statements in the book that bears his name, Jeremiah would go on to write another book so steeped in anguish that it has come to be known as, "The Lamentations of Jeremiah."

For centuries, God had repeatedly warned each generation of Israel about the danger of turning from Him. As far back as the days of Moses, those who were alive at that time had been told, "Then it shall be, if you by any means forget the Lord your God, and follow other gods, and serve them and worship them, I testify against you this day that you shall surely perish. As the nations which the Lord destroys before you, so you shall perish, because you would not be obedient to the voice of the Lord your God." (Deuteronomy 8:19-20). Generation after generation of Israelites heard the Lord's warnings. One right after another, they rejected God's Word.

When we meet Jeremiah, we find a man who would deliver God's admonitions just as his divinely inspired predecessors in prophecy had done. The difference between Jeremiah and many of the earlier prophets was that Jeremiah would himself actually see the destruction that God had promised would come to the disobedient nation. He was right there in the middle of it all. If anyone ever had a right to say, "I told you so" in regard to a matter, it would have been Jeremiah.

To say that Israel, or, more specifically, Judah, was experiencing the saddest time in its history during Jeremiah's day would probably be an understatement. Yet it's at this point that we remind ourselves that stars shine their brightest when the night is the darkest. That's why the glittering star of hope can so readily be seen throughout Jeremiah's message. Against the backdrop of the blackness of disobedience and destruction, hope's beacon shined the light of promise even on a society saturated with sin. Sadly, the people closed their eyes to the light.

This chapter's memory verse well summarizes God's mindset throughout Judah's ordeal. God wanted to give them the best. As he said through Ezekiel, "'*As* I live,' says the Lord God, 'I have no pleasure in the death of the wicked, but that the wicked turn from his way and live. Turn, turn from your evil ways! For why should you die, O house of Israel?'" (Ezekiel 33:11). Jeremiah said that God wanted to give them peace, a positive future, and hope. He had done just that for centuries. Now, the Lord's patience had been exhausted. Promised punishment became realized consequences. Jeremiah summed up the reason in the simple statement, "Jerusalem has sinned gravely, therefore she has become vile." (Lamentations 1:8). The King James Version of this verse reads, "Jerusalem hath grievously sinned; therefore she is removed."

Hope was there in Jeremiah's day, but Judah could not see it because they would not see it. It's amazing to consider how longsuffering God was with Judah. Seven different times in his book we find Jeremiah talking about how, throughout Israel's history, God had had His prophets rise up early to warn and plead with them in an effort to ward off catastrophe (Jeremiah 7:13; 7:25; 11:7; 26:5; 29:19; 32:33;

35:15). These prophets were given a full-time job to return their people to God. Why was He so longsuffering? Why did He commission His prophets to preach day after day? It was because He so very desperately wanted to bless instead of punish.

Lest we too harshly criticize Israel for their stubbornness, we would do well to be thankful for God's longsuffering toward us for we ourselves often harden our own hearts against God's will. Paul wrote, "Or do you despise the riches of His goodness, forbearance, and longsuffering, not knowing that the goodness of God leads you to repentance?" (Romans 2:4). Why is God so patient with us today? It's because He wants to give us peace (John 14:27), a future with Him in eternity, and hope that will last throughout life.

God doesn't want any souls to be lost. The proof of this is clearly seen in Jesus. "Why did my Savior come to earth?" "Because, He loved me so." "For when we were still without strength, in due time Christ died for the ungodly. For scarcely for a righteous man will one die; yet perhaps for a good man someone would even dare to die. But God demonstrates His own love toward us, in that while we were still sinners, Christ died for us." (Romans 5:6-8). As horrible as this sinful world might be and as many times as we probably ask, "Lord, how much longer can this go on?", as we observe the prevalence of sin we would do well to recall that God still wants to bless. Furthermore, just as God wanted His prophets to rise up early and tell the people of their day about the God who wanted to bless them, He has commissioned His church today to do the same (Matthew 28:19-20; Mark 16:15-16; II Timothy 2:2).

Jeremiah's message not only shows us that God wants to bless and not destroy, it reminds us that just because practically everyone around us has relinquished hope does not mean that we must as well. This truth is concisely expressed within the span of just eleven verses in Jeremiah 17. Verse 7 says, "Blessed is the man who trusts in the Lord, and whose hope is the Lord." In verse 13, Jeremiah addressed God as "the hope of Israel." Then, making his comments very personal, the mighty prophet said to the Lord, "You are my hope in the day of doom." (Jeremiah 17:17). Many in Jeremiah's day were fighting against God. Jeremiah refused to go along with the crowd. He could still see hope even though sin was seeking to shroud it.

There is no question that those of us who hope in God and walk with Him faithfully based on that hope are in the minority. It's not the first time this has been the case. In fact, throughout time, save for immediately after creation and immediately after the flood, God's faithful have been the minority. It's not bad company in which to live for we know it's not human numbers that will save us in eternity. As Solomon said, *"Though they join* forces, the wicked will not go unpunished..." (Proverbs 11:21). Moses exhorted, "You shall not follow a crowd to do evil." (Exodus 23:2).

Our hope is not measured by popular opinion. Like Jeremiah, we may stand alone, or relatively alone, amongst our family, friends, co-workers and others in our resolve to walk faithfully with the Lord. So be it. It doesn't matter what other people think of our hope. It doesn't matter what they call us, how they talk about us, etc. Because our hope is in God, our source of strength is greater than our opponents' source of criticism. Their foundation for unbelief is faulty. Our foundation is Divine. Furthermore, we don't have to rely on weak, baseless responses when we answer the unbelievers surrounding us. We can boldly state our assurance of God's existence and care for we have His perfectly inspired written Word, the Bible.

Jeremiah's book demonstrates that God wants to bless us. It also proves that we do not have to give up our hope just because many around us do. In addition, Jeremiah's words remind us that, while hope is there, it cannot be found anywhere but in God. Jeremiah 3:23 reads, "Truly, in vain *is salvation hoped for* from the hills, *and from* the multitude of mountains; truly, in the LORD our God *is* the salvation of Israel." (Jeremiah 3:23).

The history of Israel and Judah clearly proves that the gods and things of this world cannot deliver and, thus, cannot give hope. Granted, this has been touched on in earlier pages of this book. It's interesting to note, though, that God saw the need to keep reminding

His human creation of this truth. The Lord is aware of our tendency to forget. Indeed, if there's one thing we learn from history, it's that we rarely learn anything from history.

Even after Jesus came in the flesh and then ascended back to heaven after His death, burial, and resurrection, mankind's desire to follow earthly gods and earthly religions did not come to an end. Jesus had so perfectly revealed the one true God and yet many still rejected Him and continued to pursue lifeless idols and weak ideals created by men.

What salvation was Judah hoping to find in the hills and in the multitude of mountains? Maybe they thought they could hide. Perhaps they felt that the mountains would serve as walls of protection. It could be that they had deified the hills. They had done that to practically everything else (Jeremiah 11:13). For whatever reason they chose to hope in the highlands rather than in heaven, their trust was misplaced. The God who created the mountains would know their whereabouts (Psalm 90:2).

God wants to bless us, Jeremiah said. We can have hope if we will search for it. Hope in God has the potential to be so powerful that we can hold onto it even when all those around us are trying to rip it out of our hearts. True hope cannot be found in the gods or things of this world. True hope is found in the one true God alone. One final point to add in regard to Jeremiah's words about hope is that, for hope to be real, it must be combined with obedience. Again, this is a fact that has been earlier noted in this book, but let's take a fresh look at it through the eyes of Jeremiah, the man who was seeing first-hand the destruction of hope by means of disobedience.

In Jeremiah 14:8 we find Jeremiah once again addressing God as the "Hope of Israel." Look at the entire address though. "O the Hope of Israel, his Savior in time of trouble, Why should You be like a stranger in the land, and like a traveler *who* turns aside to tarry for a night? Why should You be like a man astonished, like a mighty one *who* cannot save? Yet You, O Lord, *are* in our midst, and we are called by Your name; do not leave us!" (Jeremiah 14:8-9). If Jehovah was indeed their hope, why did Jeremiah need to plead with Him to not leave? The first seven verses of the chapter show that God was already punishing them. After Jeremiah made his plea (verses 8 and 9), He heard God's answer.

> "Thus says the Lord to this people: 'Thus they have loved to wander; they have not restrained their feet. Therefore the Lord does not accept them; He will remember their iniquity now, and punish their sins.' Then the Lord said to me, 'Do not pray for this people, for *their* good. When they fast, I will not hear their cry; and when they offer burnt offering and grain offering, I will not accept them. But I will consume them by the sword, by the famine, and by the pestilence.'" (Jeremiah 14:10-12).

Jeremiah replied that the people were being told by some "prophets" that everything would be fine, there would be no destruction or famine and that they would be at peace. (Jeremiah 14:13). The people believed that message and followed those "prophets." God said, "'The prophets prophesy lies in My name. I have not sent them, commanded them, nor spoken to them; they prophesy to you a false vision, divination, a worthless thing, and the deceit of their heart.'" (Jeremiah 14:14).

The Hope of Israel was in their midst and yet the people did not enjoy the hope that He offered. Why? It was because they chose to go their own way instead of God's way. They decided to listen to men rather than the Lord. God is the only source of true hope. If it is to be found at all, it is to be found in Him. But also, the only way we will find and experience that true hope is by faithfully obeying its source.

If you haven't read the book of Jeremiah in its entirety lately, please do so soon. See the sorrow. Hear the cries of desperation. Read about the rebellion. Consider how hard-hearted men and women can become, but then meditate upon the fact that the God of hope was still there wanting to bless. It's up to mankind to respond in humble obedience to His commands.

EXERCISE YOUR MIND

True or False

1. Jeremiah has been nicknamed, "The Weeping Prophet."   T   F
2. God rarely warned the people of Israel of their sins.   T   F
3. The Lord wants to bless us.   T   F
4. Those who are faithful to God have always been in the majority in this world.   T   F
5. Others' lack of hope should not persuade us to give up our hope.   T   F

Multiple Choice

1. Jeremiah:
   A) saw the destruction of Judah first-hand;
   B) never saw Judah being punished by God;
   C) did not know Judah would be punished.

2. God's patience:
   A) will never run out;
   B) does not exist;
   C) can be exhausted.

3. God's patience:
   A) is something we should take for granted;
   B) shows His desire for us to be saved;
   C) is not evident.

4. The Israelites in Jeremiah's day:
   A) put all of their hope in God;

B) hoped for salvation from the hills and mountains;
C) followed God faithfully.

5. If we have no hope:
   A) it is because God doesn't care about us;
   B) it is because we are not looking to the one true God;
   C) it is because it is impossible to have hope.

Fill in the Blanks

(Note: All scripture quotations are taken from the New King James Version and can be found in this lesson.)

1. "Oh, that my head were _____, and my eyes a _____ of _____, that I might _____ day and night for the _____ of the daughter of my _____!"

2. "Then it shall be, if you by any means _____ the _____ your _____, and follow other _____, and _____ them and _____ them, I testify against you this day that you shall surely _____. As the _____ which the LORD _____ before you, so you shall _____, because you would not be _____ to the _____ of the _____ your _____."

3. "'*As* I _____,' says the Lord GOD, 'I have no _____ in the _____ of the _____, but that the wicked _____ from his way and _____. Turn, turn from your _____ ways! For why should you _____, O house of Israel?'"

4. "Or do you _____ the riches of His _____, _____, and _____, not knowing that the _____ of _____ leads you to _____?"

5. "For when we were still without _____, in due time _____ died for the _____. For _____ for a _____ man will one _____; yet perhaps for a _____ man someone would even _____ to die. But God

_____ His own _____ toward us, in that while we were still _____, _____ died for us."

Questions for Discussion

1. Why was Jeremiah so saddened by the sins of Israel? _____
   _____
   _____
   _____

2. Should we be saddened by sin in our day and time? If so, why? _____
   _____
   _____
   _____

3. What should we do for those who are in sin and do not know God?
   _____
   _____
   _____
   _____

4. Why did God continually warn Israel of the consequences of their disobedience? _____
   _____
   _____
   _____

5. Are we today warned about disobedience to God? Give Bible book, chapter and verse for your answer. _____

6. In a book filled with sorrow and destruction, how could Jeremiah talk about hope? _____

7. Why can't some see that God loves them and wants to bless them? _____

8. What did Paul mean by his statement in Romans 2:4? _____

9. How does the fact that God wants to bless us and save us give us hope? _____

10. How was Jeremiah able to stay strong in hope and faithful to God even in the midst of so many disobedient people? _____

11. Why should we not follow people simply because they are in the majority?

12. What are some challenges we might face when we stand up for God against unbelievers?

13. Will God reward us for our stand for Him? Give Bible book, chapter and verse for your answer.

14. Why will no one ever find true hope in anyone or anything but God?

15. Why does God insist on obedience?

_____

_____

SEARCH THE SCRIPTURES

(Note: For this section, you will find a good concordance helpful. All scripture quotations are taken from the New King James Version.)

Where is the following Bible verse located? _____

"Thus says the Lord: 'Cursed *is* the man who trusts in man and makes flesh his strength, whose heart departs from the Lord.'"

Chapter Ten

Hope in Romans

Memory Work:

" Now may the God of hope fill you with all joy and peace in believing, that you may abound in hope by the power of the Holy Spirit." (Romans 15:13)

The letter to the Romans is a wonderfully deep, multi-faceted work of Divine inspiration. When Peter made note of some of Paul's most challenging writings (II Peter 3:16), perhaps he had at least a few of the sentences in Romans in mind. The time it takes to mine the spiritual treasures in this epistle is time well spent as many themes vital to living the Christian life are addressed therein. One of those themes is that of hope.

The first reference to hope in Romans is found in the example of Abraham as cited in chapter four. Paul said of the faithful patriarch, "who, contrary to hope, in hope believed, so that he became the father of many nations, according to what was spoken, 'So shall your descendants be.'" (Romans 4:18). In the context, Paul was speaking of the promise God had made to Abraham regarding the birth of a son. Chapters 15 through 21 of Genesis tell us of how God told Abraham and his, wife, Sarah, that they would have a son, even though they were well advanced in years. Both Abraham and Sarah, though initially stunned by God's announcement, nonetheless had faith that the Lord would provide (Romans 4:19-20; Hebrews 11:11-12).

On the surface, a 90 year old woman and a 100 year old man having a child seems illogical. It is contrary to the natural order of life, thus, on the surface at least, it appears to be contrary to hope. There are many things concerning which we would give up hope after a certain point in our lives. If we're in our nineties or close to 100, we can probably give up hope of being a starting quarterback for a professional football team. At that age it's also likely that we don't need to hope that we will run a mile in less than four minutes. These feats would be contrary to nature and would not be things for which we would logically hope. The same was true for Abraham when it came to the notion of fathering a child, and yet, in spite of that, he had hope anyway because He trusted God and believed in His promises.

Many people will tell us that our hope makes no sense. They will urge us to give up on God, telling us that believing in Him is illogical and futile. Isn't that what Job's wife told him when she advised him to curse God and die (Job 2:9)? Hope in God is indeed contrary. It is contrary to the way the world thinks, but, then again, it's not the world's standard that we are trying to follow. We are seeking to follow the Lord. When tied in with belief as it was in Abraham's heart, hope defies the thinking of the world and leads us to press onward with confidence in God's promises.

In the fifth chapter of Romans we find another reference to hope. Having spoken of the joy we can have in the hope of God's glory (Romans 5:2), Paul went on to write about that which might be termed the building blocks of hope. "And not only *that*, but we also glory in tribulations, knowing that tribulation produces perseverance; and perseverance, character; and character, hope." (Romans 5:3-4).

Notice that tribulation heads this list. When we hear the word, "tribulation," our first thought is of something that is harmful. Indeed, Satan's purpose in sending trials is to harm us. Paul said, however, that we should view these difficulties in a different light. If we will open our minds and hearts with a desire to learn from our trials, they can lead to perseverance, our perseverance can build our character, and the building of our character can develop our hope.

In an earlier chapter, we considered the relationship between hope and patience. Paul's words here remind us of James' comments regarding the fact that the testing of our faith produces patience (James 1:3). Neither hope nor patience comes easily. In fact, for some of us, they seem to come harder than for others. I recall one Christian friend telling me that he does not pray for patience because he is afraid of what he might have to go through to get it.

Perhaps what we fail to see is that hope, like patience, does not just plop down into our laps at any given moment. It's not like we live the majority of our lives without hope and then one day we suddenly have it. Our hope begins when we obey the Gospel and then continues to develop through a process. Each day of our Christian walk we have hope and each day presents an opportunity for us to build our hope. Ideally, our hope is stronger today than it was yesterday and it will be stronger tomorrow than it is today. Regardless of the current state of hope in our hearts, it is present here and now at least at some level. The challenges to our faith give that hope an opportunity to grow stronger.

Take a look back at your life. Can you think of at least one time in which it seemed that all was lost? Maybe a loved one passed away. Perhaps you went through financial difficulties. Maybe you suffered an illness or injury. Whatever the challenge was, you made it through. Your hope in God was rewarded and now you are stronger than you were then. Perhaps at the time you wondered how you would make it. Now, in retrospect, you see how you made it. The Lord was with you, blessing you and watching over you. That challenge prepared you for the next one. As you experienced God's care through each ensuing challenge, your hope got stronger. Even though you might not have seen your hope building at the time of a trial, you can look back now and see evidence of its development within you.

Through hope, we are able to see Satan's stumbling blocks as God's stepping stones. As our hope grows, so does our personal spirituality as well as our influence on those around us. Satan wants to bring us down, but our hope lifts us up. As Romans 5:5 says, "hope does not disappoint." The reason it does not disappoint is because of the ever present love of God about which we learn in the Bible and which we experience in His daily providential care.

The eighth chapter of Romans contains a plurality of verses that speak of hope. The immediate context of these verses begins in verse 18. Paul first wrote of the suffering that they were enduring but then contrasted that with the glory that faithful Christians will one day know. In verse 19 he spoke of waiting. In verse 20 he used the word, "hope." In verse 21, he wrote of deliverance. In verse 23 he again made a reference to waiting. Once again, hope is associated with patience. The rewards for hope here stated are glory and deliverance.

Now we come to Romans 8:24-25. "For we were saved in this hope, but hope that is seen is not hope; for why does one still hope for what he sees? But if we hope for what we do not see, we eagerly wait for *it* with perseverance." These brethren were suffering greatly for the faith. Ensuing verses continued the exhortation to remain strong as Paul reminded them of God's care and love. The challenge was that, while they could see the daily work of Satan via the persecution and hardships, they could not yet see the glory and eternal deliverance of God. They would have to wait for these eternal blessings. They would have to endure. They would have to hope. Their time for going home to be with the Lord would come. In the meantime, God would provide what they needed to stay strong. He would not forsake them. It's a message that still rings true today.

The word translated, "eagerly wait" in verse 25 is rarely used in the New Testament. Each time it is used, it has reference to waiting for or looking toward eternity (Romans 8:19,23,25; I Corinthians 1:7; Galatians 5:5; Philippians 3:20; Hebrews 9:28). It indicates a longing for the Lord's coming to take the faithful to heaven. To illustrate this, imagine a mother and father who, a number of years earlier, had watched their son leave home to join the military. We could even imagine him serving a tour of duty in a dangerous, battle stricken area of the world. During that time, his parents would have thought about him, prayed for him and, above all, greatly longed for the day when they could see him again. Now, having been gone for that lengthy period, the son is coming back. Imagine the look in the parents' eyes and the hope and excitement in their hearts as they anticipate their son's return. You can almost see them staring intently at the scene before them, anxiously waiting for just that first glimpse of their beloved child. It's this type of longing that is depicted in Paul's words, "eagerly wait." Faithful Christians want to go home to be with the Lord. We get excited about the prospect of eternity in heaven. We watch. We pray. We wait. We hope. God will reward the faithful. There is good reason for our hope.

In the next reference to hope in Romans, we find Paul speaking of rejoicing in hope (Romans 12:12). These words are couched in a series of brief exhortations to Christians that takes up practically the entire chapter. This is actually a participial phrase that ties in with the previous verses. That being the case, Paul was saying that we should heed all of his inspired exhortations while rejoicing in hope. We can serve God, encourage one another, and work hard while we rejoice in hope for we know that we are honoring God in our deeds. Whatever task is at hand, we should remember that it is an opportunity to glorify God. This is ample reason to rejoice. When you add to it the fact that each opportunity for service is also an opportunity to demonstrate our hope so that others can be built up and brought closer to God, the reasons to rejoice are multiplied.

Romans 15:4 contains another reference to hope. Paul wrote, "For whatever things were written before were written for our learning, that we through the patience and comfort of the Scriptures might have hope." Much has already been said about the value of the Scriptures in serving as the foundation for hope. This passage reaffirms that truth but also brings back to mind the correlation between hope, patience, and comfort.

The final mention of hope in Romans is this chapter's memory verse. It is found toward the end of the epistle as Paul was wrapping up his missive to the Roman Christians. To this point in the epistle, Paul has given an example of hope in the person of Abraham, has shown the building blocks of hope, has demonstrated the power of hope in aiding Christians when we are being tried by Satan, has reminded his readers of the need to rejoice in hope, and has exalted God's Word as the source of hope. Now, as the letter comes to a conclusion, it seems that Paul was summarizing his comments on hope in this passage.

Note that the beginning focus in Romans 15:13 is on the fact that the Lord is the God of hope. In the Bible, we see clearly that God wants to bless. This is evident as far back as the Garden of Eden. Rather than giving up on mankind when he sinned, God instead held out hope for His human creation by announcing His plan to redeem our souls (Genesis 3:15). When Israel cried out to God for deliverance from Egyptian bondage, their pleas were heard by the God of hope and He delivered them from their oppressors (Exodus 3-14). Centuries later He brought this deliverance back to mind when he said through the Psalmist, "I *am* the LORD your God, who brought you out of the land of Egypt; open your mouth wide, and I will fill it." (Psalm 81:10). As He intended to bless Israel with freedom from captivity, so also He would bless them with all that they needed in the Psalmist's day.

In the New Testament, God is portrayed as the one who has always been very near and readily available to humanity. This is seen in the coming of Jesus but it was also stated by Paul when he said that God is not far from any one of us (Acts 17:27). Going back to the Old Testament, we read the Lord saying that He takes no pleasure in the death of the wicked (Ezekiel 33:11), while in the New Testament it is said that He "desires all men to be saved and to come to the knowledge of the truth." (I Timothy 2:4).

Verse after verse could be cited to demonstrate that God wants to give us His best here and save us in eternity. In that regard, He is the God of hope. He does not want us to be lost. He does not want to abandon us. He wants to help us.

The famous 18th century preacher, Jonathan Edwards, once delivered a sermon entitled, "Sinners In the Hands of an Angry God."

In that fiery message, Edwards painted God as one who dangles sinful mankind over the fires of hell, prepared to drop us at any moment. While it is true that God will cast the disobedient into everlasting punishment (Matthew 25:46), His desire is for all to be saved. Based on the Bible's description of God, we would better picture Him as trying to hold us up, away from the flames of damnation. If we are lost in eternity, it will not be because God takes delight in punishment. It will be in spite of all that God has done to save us. Hell is a reality, but so is heaven. God wants to bless us with heaven. He holds out hope for eternity with Him because He is the God of hope.

Look at Romans 15:13 and see what this God of hope provides for us to encourage our hope. He offers peace and joy through faith. The hope that is associated with this peace and joy is no ordinary hope. It is abundant hope. Not only does the God of hope want to bless us, He blesses us far beyond what we can imagine. Jesus said He came to give the abundant life. (John 10:10). Paul wrote of "Him who is able to do exceedingly abundantly above all that we ask or think, according to the power that works in us." (Ephesians 3:20). We can abound in hope because we serve the God of hope.

I urge you to go back and read the letter to the Romans from the perspective of a Christian who is weary and worn from Satan's attacks. Doing so, you will see how much importance the Holy Spirit, through Paul, placed on hope. It can sustain us, lift us up, and, ultimately, lead us to eternal salvation as through that hope we draw closer to God and become more committed to doing His will.

EXERCISE YOUR MIND

True or False

1. Abraham had hope, even though fathering a child at his age seemed illogical.　　T　　F

2. Once a person becomes a Christian, he or she never again has any difficulties in this life. T   F
3. Hope does not just suddenly appear over night. T   F
4. God permits challenges because He wants to destroy us. T   F
5. God wants to bless us. T   F

Multiple Choice

1. Abraham had hope in God:
   A) because of his faith;
   B) because he had seen how God had blessed him;
   C) both A and B.

2. Job's wife:
   A) was supportive;
   B) trusted God;
   C) told Job to curse God and die.

3. Satan wants tribulations to:
   A) make us stronger;
   B) destroy us;
   C) help us love God more.

4. Our God is:
   A) the God of hope;
   B) very distant and unconcerned about us;
   C) not as powerful as Satan.

5. God:
   A) gives us nothing;
   B) gives us His best;
   C) gives us as little as possible.

Fill in the Blanks

(Note: All scripture quotations are taken from the New King James Version and can be found in this lesson.)
1. "Who, _____ to hope, in hope _____, so that he became the _____ of many _____, according to what was spoken, 'So shall your _____ be.'"
2. "And not only *that*, but we also _____ in _____, knowing that _____ produces _____; and _____, _____; and _____, _____."
3. "For we were _____ in this hope, but hope that is _____ is not hope; for why does one still _____ for what he sees? But if we hope for what we do not _____, we _____ wait for *it* with _____."
4. "For _____ things were _____ before were _____ for our learning, that we through the _____ and _____ of the _____ might have _____."
5. "I *am* the _____ your _____, who _____ you out of the land of _____; open your _____ wide, and I will _____ it."

Questions for Discussion

1. Why does hoping in God make no sense to some people? _____
   _____
   _____
   _____

2. Read Mark 10:27. What did Jesus mean when He said this?
   _____

_____
_____

3. What does it mean to persevere? _____
_____
_____
_____

4. How can we demonstrate perseverance in our walk with God?
_____
_____
_____

5. What is character? _____
_____
_____
_____

6. How do tribulations develop perseverance? _____
_____
_____
_____

7. How does perseverance build character? _____
_____
_____
_____

8. How does the building of character develop hope? _____

9. In what ways does hope save us (Romans 8:24)? _____

10. Should we be looking forward to the Lord's return in judgment? Why or why not? _____

11. Why would someone not be looking forward to the Lord's return in judgment? _____

12. In what ways has God demonstrated that He is the God of hope?

13. Considering that we so often fail God, why does He want to bless us?

14. What did Paul mean when he said that God is not far from each one of us (Acts 17:27)?

15. What does it mean to abound in hope?

SEARCH THE SCRIPTURES

(Note: For this section, you will find a good concordance helpful. All scripture quotations are taken from the New King James Version.)

Where is the following Bible verse located? _____

"Now faith is the substance of things hoped for, the evidence of things not seen."

Chapter Eleven

Inspiring Hope in Others

Memory Work:

"So *shall* the knowledge of wisdom *be* to your soul; If you have found *it,* there is a prospect, and your hope will not be cut off." (Proverbs 24:14)

Much has been said in this book about the many ways in which hope helps us overcome the world. Whether we are discouraged, heartbroken, distressed, or worn and wearied by the trials of life, hope can bring us back up. We know that's true, but what about those around us who are not aware of this fact? In chapter five we talked about utilizing the defense of our hope as an evangelistic tool. Since, ultimately, our desire is to win souls, in this chapter we will discuss ways in which we can inspire hope in those who do not have it. Typically, this will be something we do in our interactions with non-Christians, but many times our own spiritual brothers and sisters find themselves in need of a boost. How can we help them build, or perhaps even regain, their hope?

Paul told the Philippian church, "Finally, my brethren, rejoice in the Lord. For me to write the same things to you *is* not tedious, but for you *it is* safe." (Philippians 3:1). Peter wrote, "For this reason I will not be negligent to remind you always of these things, though you know and are established in the present truth. Yes, I think it is right, as long as I am in this tent, to stir you up by reminding *you*." (II Peter 1:12-13). Both inspired writers knew the value of repetition when it came to being able to commit truth to memory. With that principle in mind, let's again state a principle that has been written many times in this book. The Word of God is the source of hope that strengthens us here on earth and leads us toward heaven.

In the Bible we read of some who offered false hope. In I Kings 22 we find the account of King Ahab of Israel and King Jehoshaphat of Judah joining forces to battle the nation of Syria. Ahab was a wicked man who had paid men to tell him what he wanted to hear. One of those charlatans was Zedekiah. He told Ahab that he would obliterate the Syrians (I Kings 22:11). The only trouble was that he was not a prophet of God. Micaiah, the true prophet of God, told Ahab that he would not return from the battle (I Kings 22:28). Ensuing verses tell us that Ahab was indeed killed in the war against the Syrians. Zedekiah had given him hope, but it was false hope. God's Word is the only real source of hope. That's why, when we talk about inspiring hope in others, we must be sure that in our exhortations we rely on the only book that has been inspired by God, the Bible. In so doing, the words are not ours. They are the Lord's.

Before considering some suggestions for inspiring hope in others, let's briefly look at how NOT to do it. For this discussion we look at Job and his interaction with his friends after Job had lost every physical blessing except his life.

Job was despondent. Who among us wouldn't be?! He said, "My days are swifter than a weaver's shuttle, and are spent without hope." (Job 7:6). Later he asked, "Where then *is* my hope? As for my hope, who can see it? (Job 17:15). His friends heard his laments and made an assumption that was based on a false premise. The false premise was that suffering is always caused by disobedience to God. The assumption, then, was that Job must have done something to displease the Lord. The bulk of their responses to him were couched in that assumption. Thus, their words did not comfort or inspire hope. Rather, they drove him deeper into despair. At one point Job even told them, "But you forgers of lies, you *are* all worthless physicians." (Job 13:4).

From the standpoint of what NOT to do to inspire hope in others, let's observe from Job's friends that they were not really listening to him. Granted, they sat in silence by his side for seven days and nights (Job 2:13). It would seem that they were of more help to him in their silence than in their speeches. What they heard Job say when he finally began to express his grief led them to begin accusing him of wrongdoing. They weren't listening to him. Instead, they were bent on telling him what they thought. Eliphaz, one of Job's friends, said, "Who can withhold himself from speaking?" (Job 4:2). Zophar, another friend, said, "Therefore my anxious thoughts make me answer, because of the turmoil within me." (Job 20:2). Both men felt that they just had to say something and what they had to say came out in the form of criticism.

James wrote, "So then, my beloved brethren, let every man be swift to hear, slow to speak, slow to wrath." (James 1:19). If we are going to be of help to those who are lacking or are weak in hope, we are going to have to open our ears and listen to them. Why are they feeling hopeless? What scriptures would apply to them in their present situation? We can only know the answers to these questions if our ears and hearts are open. Far too often we fail to really hear a person because we are too busy formulating our answers while that individual is speaking. Job's friends show us the danger of having our ears closed when interacting with someone whose hope is either dying or completely gone. They had a great opportunity to pray to God for their friend, to speak words of faith to him, and to encourage him to keep trusting in God. So many beautiful words of hope could have filled Job's heart, but, instead, all he got were words of unjust condemnation. Poor listening on our part plays a major role in discouraging rather than encouraging hope in others.

At the heart of inspiring hope in others is reminding them that God is in their midst, no matter how dark their night might be. Jeremiah said, "Do not be a terror to me; You *are* my hope in the day of doom." (Jeremiah 17:17). All the verses earlier cited plus many more should be pointed out to the hope-starved individual to help him or her see that the God who was there when things were going well is still present.

He walks with those who follow Him through the valley of the shadow of death (Psalm 23:4). The Psalmist sang, "And those who know Your name will put their trust in You; for You, LORD, have not forsaken those who seek You." (Psalm 9:10).

We can inspire hope in others by speaking plainly to them. Paul said, "Therefore, since we have such hope, we use great boldness of speech." (II Corinthians 3:12). In other words, we don't try to cover up God's truth when we are making the effort to help someone build hope. There's just way too much fluff and nonsense being spouted in the name of religion today. There are many "uncertain sounds" coming from pulpits throughout the land. It's confusing people and, in their confusion, they are getting discouraged and giving up on God. While we are to speak the truth in love (Ephesians 4:15), we must be sure that the truth is spoken even when it is not popular or desired.

"For God is not *the author* of confusion but of peace, as in all the churches of the saints." (I Corinthians 14:33). God's Word is plain. Granted there are some passages that are difficult to grasp, but they are not impossible to understand. A clear and orderly discussion of the Sacred Scriptures can help a person see that God has given an obvious path to heaven in His Word.

I remember a commercial in which people were chosen at random to complete an assignment. The leader of the study started the assignment by giving each participant very confusing instructions on what they were supposed to accomplish. After about ten minutes, the study leader came into the room and gave more instructions, each of which was contrary to the first set that had been given. He repeated that after another ten minutes had passed. On hidden camera, one could see the frustration on the faces and in the actions of these participants. Eventually, they just gave up. They had lost hope of ever getting the assignment right. Could it be that some today have lost or are losing hope because of the confusion they see when they look around at the current state of what is called Christianity? Plain speech from an open Bible would solve this trouble and build hope.

We can inspire hope in others by citing examples of faithful men and women in the Bible who grew in hope despite the efforts of Satan to get them to give up. The apostle Paul suffered incredibly for the cause of Christ and yet he was a man of great hope. He told the Corinthian Christians, "*We are* hard-pressed on every side, yet not crushed; *we are* perplexed, but not in despair; persecuted, but not forsaken; struck down, but not destroyed." (II Corinthians 4:8-9). Perhaps the one in whom you are seeking to inspire hope is feeling hard-pressed, perplexed, and stricken. Study Paul's example with them to see how, even though he had those same feelings, he knew that he was not defeated. A few years after he penned the second epistle to the Corinthians, he wrote these words to Timothy: "For to this *end* we both labor and suffer reproach, because we trust in the living God, who is *the* Savior of all men, especially of those who believe." (I Timothy 4:10). His hope stayed strong through the years until, at last, it saw him home (II Timothy 4:6-8). If Paul could do it, why can't each of us? He served the same God and followed the same inspired Word as we do. Again, if he could have hope in the circumstances he faced, why can't we?

A way to inspire hope specifically in Christians who are struggling is to remind them who they are. Colossians 1:27 reads, "To them God willed to make known what are the riches of the glory of this mystery among the Gentiles: which is Christ in you, the hope of glory." Christ dwells in the Christian through His written Word, the Bible (Ephesians 3:17; Romans 10:17). A Christian is one who belongs to Christ. When one hears the Word of God (Romans 10:17), believes in Jesus as Christ (John 8:24), repents of his or her sins (Luke 13:3,5), confesses faith in Jesus as the Christ (Acts 8:36-38), and is immersed into Christ for the forgiveness of sins (Acts 2:38), he or she rises from the water a new creature, forgiven of past sins (Romans 6:3ff). At that point, the Lord adds them to His church (Acts 2:47). Christians have been bought at a price, that price being Jesus' blood (I Corinthians 6:20). That makes us "a chosen generation, a royal priesthood, a holy nation, His own special people" according to I Peter 2:9.

Sometimes people give up hope because they forget how special they are. The world keeps telling them that they don't measure up if they don't look, dress, talk, and act a certain way. To encourage those who are the brunt of such attacks, we typically remind them of their uniqueness. We remind them that they are individuals created in the image of God (Genesis 1:27). These words of encouragement have led many to break the mold and attain levels of success that many never thought possible.

In this manner, it is good for all Christians to remember who we are. We all need to keep at least a mental list of God's blessings in our hearts. Bringing this to the attention of the Christian who is wavering in his or her hope would be of great value to that brother or sister.

Finally, we can inspire hope in others simply by speaking words of encouragement to them. Solomon had something to say about the power of an encouraging word.

> "A man has joy by the answer of his mouth, and a word *spoken* in due season, how good *it is!*" (Proverbs 15:23).

> "Pleasant words *are like* a honeycomb, Sweetness to the soul and health to the bones." (Proverbs 16:24).

> "A word fitly spoken *is like* apples of gold in settings of silver." (Proverbs 25:11).

We should all strive to be great encouragers like the apostle Paul. As we read his epistles, we find that he complimented and expressed confidence whenever he could. Paul told the Corinthian Christians, "not boasting of things beyond measure, *that is,* in other men's labors, but having hope, *that* as your faith is increased, we shall be greatly enlarged by you in our sphere." (II Corinthians 10:15). Even though he had had to address so much error in the church at Corinth, Paul nonetheless held out hope for them that they would grow out of their spiritual infancy and grow in the faith. Take a look at each of Paul's letters and make note of the words of encouragement that he wrote by inspiration of the Holy Spirit. Notice also how he continually wished God's blessings of grace and peace upon his readers.

There are few joys that can excel the kind words that someone offers to us. As a pre-teen before I obeyed the Gospel, I was approached one Sunday by the elderly preacher at the congregation where my family worshipped. He took me aside and said, "You're going to be a great Christian some day." I'm not sharing that because I feel I am a great Christian. I am far from that. I'm sharing it because it shows the power of the encouraging word. Over 40 years later, my heart and hope are still lifted by this kind brother's thoughtful comment and his words inspire me to press on in my spiritual growth.

May we all have our eyes and hearts open to the opportunities to build hope in others. They surround us every day. May we then have the compassion of Jesus and see those who are fainting and scattered abroad as sheep without a shepherd (Matthew 9:36-38) and may we raise their hope by opening God's Word and studying it with them.

EXERCISE YOUR MIND

True or False

1. We never need to be reminded of spiritual truths. T F
2. There is no such thing as false hope. T F
3. Job's friends were very helpful to him. T F
4. God is always near. T F
5. We should clearly present God's truth in love. T F

Multiple Choice

1. Zedekiah told Ahab:
   A) the truth;
   B) what he wanted to hear;
   C) that he would die in battle.

2. Job's friends:
   A) were very supportive;
   B) were of great help to Job;
   C) did not listen well.

3. Man-made religious doctrines:
   A) confuse people;
   B) are approved by God;
   C) are acceptable because no one can really know the truth anyway.

4. Christians:
   A) are a special people;
   B) have been bought by the blood of Jesus Christ;
   C) both A and B.

5. Every time he could, the apostle Paul seemed to enjoy:
   A) criticizing others;
   B) encouraging others;
   C) ignoring others.

Fill in the Blanks

(Note: All scripture quotations are taken from the New King James Version and can be found in this lesson.)
1. "Finally, my brethren, _____ in the _____. For me to _____ the _____ things to you *is* not _____, but for you *it is* _____."

Inspiring Hope in Others

2. "So then, my _____ brethren, let every man be _____ to _____, _____ to _____, _____ to _____."
3. "And those who _____ Your _____ will put their _____ in _____; for You, _____, have not _____ those who _____ You."
4. "Therefore, since we have such _____, we use great _____ of _____."
5. "*We are* _____ on every side, yet not _____; *we are* _____, but not in _____; _____, but not _____; _____ _____, but not _____."

Questions for Discussion

1. Does the fact that a Christian can struggle with hope mean that he or she is weak in the faith? Explain your answer. _____
_____
_____
_____

2. Why do we sometimes lose hope? _____
_____
_____
_____

3. Why is it helpful for us to be reminded of the truths of God's Word? _____
_____
_____
_____

4. What other Bible examples of those who promised false hope come to mind? _____

_____

_____

_____

5. What are some modern-day examples of promises of false hope?

_____

_____

_____

_____

6. Why do people put their hope in people and things rather than in God? _____

_____

_____

_____

7. How can we improve our listening skills? _____

_____

_____

_____

8. What are the benefits to the people to whom we are talking when we listen carefully to them? _____

_____

_____

_____

9. What benefits do we receive by listening carefully to others? _____

10. What blessings come from knowing that God is always near to us as we follow Him faithfully? _____

11. Why is the religious division and confusion that is prevalent today destructive to hope? _____

12. Name some of the blessings that we enjoy as Christians. _____

13. Who can you cite as other Bible examples of hope? _____

14. Can you think of a Christian you know or have known who is or was a great example of hope? Why did that person come to mind?

_____
_____
_____

15. What one verse in the Bible would you turn to first in your effort to inspire hope in others? _____

_____
_____
_____

SEARCH THE SCRIPTURES

(Note: For this section, you will find a good concordance helpful. All scripture quotations are taken from the New King James Version.)

Where is the following Bible verse located? _____

"Finally then, brethren, we urge and exhort in the Lord Jesus that you should abound more and more, just as you received from us how you ought to walk and to please God."

Chapter Twelve

Jesus' Victory - The Reason for Our Hope

Memory Work:

"Blessed *be* the God and Father of our Lord Jesus Christ, who according to His abundant mercy has begotten us again to a living hope through the resurrection of Jesus Christ from the dead." (I Peter 1:3)

Death has the potential to be the ultimate tool of defeat. Since it was introduced to the world in the Garden of Eden, death has been the unwelcome guest in untold numbers of homes. How many tears of sorrow have been shed, how many screams of anguish have pierced the air, how many hearts have been shattered as the result of watching loved ones pass from this life to the next through the portal of death? Everyone reading this book has felt its chilling presence as it swept past us to touch parents, brothers, sisters, children, spouses and others we hold dear. One day it will come to us as well. One day the lifeless body in the casket will be ours. One day the weeping and mourning, the heartfelt singing of hymns, the preacher's oration, and the writing on the tombstone will all be for us. "And as it is appointed for men to die once, but after this the judgment." (Hebrews 9:27).

Death has the POTENTIAL to be the ultimate tool of defeat, but it does not have to be because Jesus gained the victory over death. As

Hebrews 2:14-15 states, "Inasmuch then as the children have partaken of flesh and blood, He Himself likewise shared in the same, that through death He might destroy him who had the power of death, that is, the devil, and release those who through fear of death were all their lifetime subject to bondage."

Jesus' victory over death was the culmination of God's plan that He had announced all the way back in the days of Adam and Eve. Said the Lord to the serpent, "And I will put enmity between you and the woman, and between your seed and her Seed; He shall bruise your head, and you shall bruise His heel." (Genesis 3:15). From that point on in the Bible we find inspired prophet after inspired prophet speaking of the One in God's plan who would deal a crushing blow to Satan. That One was Jesus, the eternal Word (John 1:1), who became flesh and dwelt among us (John 1:14), who lived a perfect life (I Peter 2:22), died on the cross (Luke 23:46) and then rose from the dead, a victor over Satan.

No words are so beautiful as those which were spoken by two men in shining garments on a Sunday morning after the Jewish Passover nearly 2,000 years ago. Here's how Luke describes the scene:

> "Now on the first *day* of the week, very early in the morning, they, and certain *other women* with them, came to the tomb bringing the spices which they had prepared. But they found the stone rolled away from the tomb. Then they went in and did not find the body of the Lord Jesus. And it happened, as they were greatly perplexed about this, that behold, two men stood by them in shining garments. Then, as they were afraid and bowed *their* faces to the earth, they said to them, 'Why do you seek the living among the dead? He is not here, but is risen! Remember how He spoke to you when He was still in Galilee, saying, 'The Son of Man must be delivered into the hands of sinful men, and be crucified, and the third day rise again.'" (Luke 24:1-7).

Within weeks after His resurrection, Jesus ascended back to heaven (Acts 1:9). Not many days thereafter, His apostles stood in the streets of Jerusalem and the first Gospel sermon was delivered. Speaking of Jesus, Peter declared, "whom God raised up, having loosed the pains of death, because it was not possible that He should be held by it." (Acts 2:24). Death could not hold Jesus in the tomb. Our Lord was, and is, more powerful than death. The death, burial, and resurrection of the Christ, though foolish sounding to the worldly heart, is nonetheless the power of God to those who are following the Lord (I Corinthians 1:18).

The New Testament contains over 200 references to the resurrection of Jesus. Every New Testament book but the book of James speaks of Jesus' resurrection. Peter tied in Jesus' resurrection with our hope when he said, "who through Him believe in God, who raised Him from the dead and gave Him glory, so that your faith and hope are in God." (I Peter 1:21). As seen in this lesson's memory verse, earlier in that same letter Peter had said that the resurrection of Jesus has begotten us again to a living hope. The King James Version calls it a "lively hope." It is a hope as lively as the inspired Word that tells us about Jesus' victory (Hebrews 4:12). It is a hope as alive as the Savior Himself.

Our Lord's victory over death carries with it several powerful meanings for those who obey God's will. Each meaning feeds the hope within our hearts.

Jesus' victory means that God is more powerful than Satan. That seems like such an obvious statement, and yet, how often do we find ourselves questioning God's ability to take care of us? How many times have we felt that the pull of the world was stronger than the force of righteousness? How frequently have we personally succumbed to Satan's lie that he is stronger than God and that, thus, we should listen to him and enjoy the pleasures of this life that we can see rather than follow a God we cannot see?

Every argument made against God is a lie. The idea that He does not exist is a lie. The notion that if He does exist then He is not all powerful is a lie. The thought that if He does exist then He doesn't really care for His human creation is a lie. Each of these, plus every other fabrication like them, has its origin in Satan, the father of lies (John 8:44).

Why does Satan want us to believe lies about God? Why does he want to intimidate us into doubting and even rejecting God? It's because he knows he is inferior to God. He knows he cannot undo what Jesus has done. He knows the Gospel will save our souls. He knows we can have the hope of heaven in our hearts. All he has left are his lies and even he knows that his lies are weaker than the hope of a faithful Christian.

Jesus' victory means that we serve the living Savior. While world religions seek their lifeless gods, we follow the One who overcame death and who reigns in His spiritual kingdom. "I *am* He who lives, and was dead, and behold, I am alive forevermore," He declared from heaven's portals some four to six decades after His death, burial and resurrection (Revelation 1:18). We serve the living Savior who, after His resurrection and return to heaven, became our Mediator (I Timothy 2:5) and Advocate (I John 2:1). We serve the risen Savior who ever lives to make intercession for us (Hebrews 7:25).

When we go to the Father in prayer, we do so through our living Savior (Romans 7:25). Praying "in Jesus' name" when we go to God is not uttering an empty phrase. It is praying according to God's will (I John 5:14), but it is also acknowledging the existence of our risen Lord. "In Jesus' name" means by His authority; and yet, if Jesus is dead, He no longer has authority. If He is dead, He was defeated by Satan and is thus inferior to Satan. But Jesus is alive. He has authority (Matthew 28:18). He has been given power, and glory, and a kingdom (Daniel 7:14; I Peter 1:21).

Jesus' victory means that we have a captain who has led the way through the veil of death. Hebrews 2:10 refers to Jesus as "the captain of their salvation." The word, "captain" denotes one who leads the way or blazes a trail.

None of us reading this material personally knows death. We have walked through the valley with loved ones and perhaps have even come close to death ourselves, but we have yet to peer beyond its veil. Jesus has been there and He came back a conqueror, blazing the trail of victory that we ourselves can now walk because of Him.

Jesus' victory means that mankind can be victorious. We don't have to succumb to Satan. We don't have to be in bondage to the fear of death. Jesus defeated death. Through Him, we can as well. This is such a powerful and hope-inspiring thought that the entire final chapter of this volume is devoted to it.

Jesus said to mournful Martha, "I am the resurrection and the life. He who believes in Me, though he may die, he shall live. And whoever lives and believes in Me shall never die. Do you believe this?" (John 11:25-26). She answered that she believed He was the Christ, the Son of God, who had been promised, but she apparently did not fully grasp the depth of Jesus' statement. Soon she would see His power as she witnessed Him raise her brother, Lazarus from the dead (John 11:43-44). She was probably also one of those who saw many formerly deceased friends back among the living after Jesus Himself rose (Matthew 27:52-53). She saw His power to raise the dead. She saw the power of Him having been raised from the dead. The essence of His statement to her upon the death of her brother was that He is the source of resurrection and life.

I Timothy 1:1 refers to Jesus as our hope. A literal rendering of the phrase says that Jesus is "the hope of us." He is THE hope of us. There is no hope outside of Him for there is no salvation outside of Him (Acts 4:12).

The next time you get discouraged, dear Christian, think about Jesus. Hebrews 4:15 says of Him, "For we do not have a High Priest who cannot sympathize with our weaknesses, but was in all *points* tempted as *we are, yet* without sin." Jesus was tempted (Matthew 4:1ff). He was surrounded by sin (Matthew 15:3; John 9:41; et al.). He was threatened (John 10:31). One of His loved ones got sick and died (John 11:3,14).

He was lied about (Matthew 26:60-61). He was mocked (Luke 22:63). His friends forsook Him in His time of greatest need (Mark 14:50). One of His apostles betrayed Him (Matthew 26:14-16). One of His closest friends vehemently denied even knowing Him (Matthew 26:74).

Do we ourselves not struggle with many of these same trials? Have you ever been tempted? Is sin all around you? Have you ever been threatened for your faith? It need not be a death threat like Jesus faced in order for it to be a legitimate threat. Sometimes our jobs are threatened because of our stand for God. Have you ever had a loved one get sick and die? Has anyone ever told a lie about you? Have you been mocked for your faith? Have any of your friends ever abandoned you or tried to harm you in some way?

Any one of these trials in our lives could cause us to give up hope. Even a moment of trial in any of these areas can lead to discouragement. Some of you reading this book have experienced or perhaps are experiencing more than just a moment's trial though. Some of you have seen trial after trial come into your life. You have been hurt. You have wondered why you should bother to have hope. Like Asaph of old, who found himself in similar straits, perhaps you have said, "Surely I have cleansed my heart *in* vain, and washed my hands in innocence. For all day long I have been plagued, and chastened every morning." (Psalm 73:13-14).

Jesus faced life's trials and overcame them. Jesus died and conquered death in His resurrection. He did all of this so that you and I can have hope. He did all this so that you and I can have the hope that every day that we wake up we will find our Lord near. He did all this so that you and I can have the hope that every day brings us that much closer to the peace and rest of eternity in heaven.

I often tell people that I cannot enjoy reading mysteries. The reason for this is because I always want to go to the final pages first so I can see how things turn out. In regard to spiritual matters, both you and I can go to the final pages and see how things turn out. The Bible says that, in the end, God wins. Because of Jesus, those who walk with Him to the end win as well. "Blessed *are* those who do His commandments, that they may have the right to the tree of life, and may enter through the gates into the city." (Revelation 22:14). His victory brings hope of our own victory that we can have through Him.

EXERCISE YOUR MIND

true or false

1. Jesus' victory over death means that we too can have victory over death. T F
2. God's plan for delivering mankind from sin was first announced in the Garden of Eden. T F
3. Satan is more powerful than God. T F
4. Satan always tells the truth. T F
5. Jesus is the resurrection and the life. T F

multiple choice

1. Jesus:
   A) was defeated by Satan;
   B) delivered Satan a crushing blow;
   C) did not have any effect on Satan.

2. To the worldly mind, the death, burial, and resurrection of Jesus is:
   A) true;
   B) sensible;
   C) foolishness.

3. To the Christian, the death, burial, and resurrection of Jesus is:
   A) the power of God;
   B) foolishness;
   C) impossible.

4. Because of Jesus' resurrection, we can have a hope that is:
   A) dead;
   B) living;
   C) a mere guess at best.

5. Jesus:
   A) is dead;
   B) never really died;
   C) is alive.

Fill in the Blanks

(Note: All scripture quotations are taken from the New King James Version and can be found in this lesson.)

1. "Inasmuch then as the _____ have partaken of _____ and _____, He Himself likewise _____ in the same, that through _____ He might _____ him who had the _____ of death, that is, the _____, and _____ those who through _____ of death were all their _____ subject to _____."

2. "And I will put _____ between _____ and the _____, and between your _____ and her _____; He shall _____ your _____, and you shall _____ His _____."

3. "I am He who _____, and was _____, and behold, I am alive _____."

4. "I am the _____ and the _____. He who _____ in Me, though he may _____, he shall _____. And whoever _____ and _____ in Me shall never die. Do you _____ this?"

5. "For we do not have a _____ _____ who cannot _____ with our _____, but was in all points _____ as *we are, yet* without _____."

Questions for Discussion

1. In general, does mankind fear death? If so, why?

2. What are some of the ways that we demonstrate our fear of death?

3. Can we overcome the fear of death? If so, how?

4. How does the perfect life of Jesus give us hope?

5. How does the death, burial, and resurrection of Jesus give us hope?

140   Jesus' Victory - The Reason for Our Hope

6. What evidence do we have that Jesus rose from the dead? _____
   _____
   _____
   _____

7. In what way or ways did the serpent bruise the heel of the promised Seed? _____
   _____
   _____
   _____

8. In what way or ways did the promised Seed bruise the head of the serpent? _____
   _____
   _____
   _____

9. Why was it not possible for Jesus to be held by death? _____
   _____
   _____
   _____

10. Why do some consider the death, burial, and resurrection of Jesus to be foolishness? _____
    _____
    _____
    _____

Jesus' Victory -The Reason for Our Hope

11. In what sense is the death, burial, and resurrection the power of God? _____
_____
_____
_____

12. Why is it important that our hope be a living or lively hope? _____
_____
_____
_____

13. What are some of the blessings Christians enjoy as the result of serving the living Savior? _____
_____
_____
_____

14. Why is the statement found in Hebrews 4:15 so important to Christians? _____
_____
_____
_____

15. Was Jesus ever discouraged? If so, how did He handle the discouragement? _____
_____
_____
_____

SEARCH THE SCRIPTURES

(Note: For this section, you will find a good concordance helpful. All scripture quotations are taken from the New King James Version.)

Where is the following Bible verse located? _____

"To this *promise* our twelve tribes, earnestly serving *God* night and day, hope to attain. For this hope's sake, King Agrippa, I am accused by the Jews."

CHAPTER THIRTEEN

Hope's Ultimate Fulfillment

Memory Work:

"Now may our Lord Jesus Christ Himself, and our God and Father, who has loved us and given *us* everlasting consolation and good hope by grace, comfort your hearts and establish you in every good word and work." (II Thessalonians 2:16-17)

The Day is coming. It will be the Day to end all days.

> "But the day of the Lord will come as a thief in the night, in which the heavens will pass away with a great noise, and the elements will melt with fervent heat; both the earth and the works that are in it will be burned up." (II Peter 3:10).

> "For the Lord Himself will descend from heaven with a shout, with the voice of an archangel, and with the trumpet of God. And the dead in Christ will rise first." (I Thessalonians 4:16).

> "Do not marvel at this; for the hour is coming in which all who are in the graves will hear His voice and come forth—those who have done good, to the resurrection of life, and those who have done evil, to the resurrection of condemnation." (John 5:28-29).

While there are many who fancy that they know when this day will be, the truth is that none of us knows. "But concerning the times and the seasons, brethren, you have no need that I should write to you. For you yourselves know perfectly that the day of the Lord so comes as a thief in the night." (I Thessalonians 5:1-2).

For some, that Day in which the Lord comes to judge us will be a day of sorrow and punishment (Matthew 25:30). But for those who faithfully follow the Lord unto death, that Day will be one of victory and rejoicing. Those who had died in the faith will rise. Those who are alive at that time will join them in the air and together the faithful will ascend to heaven's everlasting rest. "Then we who are alive *and* remain shall be caught up together with them in the clouds to meet the Lord in the air. And thus we shall always be with the Lord." (I Thessalonians 4:17).

This day of reunion with the faithful of all time and entrance into heaven itself is the ultimate fulfillment of our hope. While the hope of God's earthly care sustains us, it is the hope of heaven that lifts us up and carries us through the battle. With each tick of the clock, we get closer home (Romans 13:11).

Throughout his various court appearances, Paul spoke at great length of this hope of heaven. He told the Sadducees and Pharisees of the Jewish council, "concerning the hope and resurrection of the dead I am being judged!" (Acts 23:6). He told the Roman governor, Felix, "I have hope in God, which they themselves also accept, that there will be a resurrection of *the* dead, both of *the* just and *the* unjust." (Acts 24:15). He stated to King Agrippa, "And now I stand and am judged for the hope of the promise made by God to our fathers." (Acts 26:6).

Throughout his epistles, Paul spoke at great length of this hope of heaven. "For we through the Spirit eagerly wait for the hope of righteousness by faith." (Galatians 5:5). He wrote to the Philippian church of his earnest expectation and hope (Philippians 1:20). He had the hope of being in heaven with those who had obeyed the Gospel he taught them (I Thessalonians 2:19). He was "looking for the blessed hope and glorious appearing of our great God and Savior Jesus Christ." (Titus 2:13). And then there is the fifteenth chapter of

First Corinthians in which we read Paul's definitive defense of the resurrection. No section of Sacred Scripture fires the excitement about our resurrection and inspires our hope for heaven quite like the words found there.

The foundation of the discussion in First Corinthians 15 is the Gospel message found in verses 3-4. "For I delivered to you first of all that which I also received: that Christ died for our sins according to the Scriptures, and that He was buried, and that He rose again the third day according to the Scriptures." After laying the foundation and then affirming that Jesus proved Himself to be alive to the apostles, to many others, and then to Paul himself, the apostle to the Gentiles proceeded to present the evidence for the resurrection.

All of the evidence applies to both Jesus' resurrection and ours. Resurrection is a fact. If not, then Jesus is still dead (verse 13). If not, then the message of salvation is worthless (verse 14). If not, then the apostles were all liars (verse 15). If resurrection is not a fact, then there is no hope in Christ and Christians are of all people most pitiable (verse 19).

Still in First Corinthians 15, we find that death is going to be destroyed (verse 26) and the righteous are going to be raised with incorruptible bodies (verses 42-44). "Behold, I tell you a mystery: We shall not all sleep, but we shall all be changed - in a moment, in the twinkling of an eye, at the last trumpet. For the trumpet will sound, and the dead will be raised incorruptible, and we shall be changed. For this corruptible must put on incorruption, and this mortal *must* put on immortality." (verses 51-53).

Now we come to the zenith of Paul's message about the resurrection.

"So when this corruptible has put on incorruption, and this mortal has put on immortality, then shall be brought to pass the saying that is written: 'Death is swallowed up in victory.' 'O Death, where *is* your sting? O Hades, where *is* your victory?' The sting of death *is* sin, and the strength of sin *is* the law. But thanks *be* to God, who gives us the victory through our Lord Jesus Christ." (verses 54-57).

Can you not close your eyes and feel the comfort and hope pouring forth from these precious words? The specter of death that haunted us through life will one day be swallowed up in victory. Its painful sting will become impotent. The righteous shall pass from the darkness of sorrow, sin and suffering into the light of eternal joy.

On the other side awaits the glory of heaven. "And God will wipe away every tear from their eyes; there shall be no more death, nor sorrow, nor crying. There shall be no more pain, for the former things have passed away." (Revelation 21:4).

"But I saw no temple in it, for the Lord God Almighty and the Lamb are its temple. The city had no need of the sun or of the moon to shine in it, for the glory of God illuminated it. The Lamb *is* its light. And the nations of those who are saved shall walk in its light, and the kings of the earth bring their glory and honor into it. Its gates shall not be shut at all by day (there shall be no night there). And they shall bring the glory and the honor of the nations into it. But there shall by no means enter it anything that defiles, or causes an abomination or a lie, but only those who are written in the Lamb's Book of Life." (Revelation 21:22-27).

The crystal clear river of water of life is there as is the tree of life (Revelation 22:1-2). "There shall be no night there: They need no lamp nor light of the sun, for the Lord God gives them light. And they shall reign forever and ever." (Revelation 22:5).

This message of our resurrection and the promise of heaven for the righteous fuels the flame of hope within our hearts. We know that we can endure here because of what God has waiting for the righteous there. Indeed, "heaven will surely be worth it all."

I can think of no better way to end this book on hope than with the exhortation given by Peter in his first epistle.

Hope's Ultimate Fulfillment

"Therefore gird up the loins of your mind, be sober, and rest *your* hope fully upon the grace that is to be brought to you at the revelation of Jesus Christ; as obedient children, not conforming yourselves to the former lusts, *as* in your ignorance; but as He who called you *is* holy, you also be holy in all *your* conduct, because it is written, 'Be holy, for I am holy.'" (I Peter 1:13-16).

It's not always easy to wait for something we are eager to have. Solomon wrote, "Hope deferred makes the heart sick, but *when* the desire comes, *it is* a tree of life." (Proverbs 13:12). But what God has awaiting the faithful in heaven is worth any challenges we might have to overcome in this life.

Peter said to be ready to take on the world. To "gird up" means to be prepared. We need to prepare our minds by channeling our thoughts toward that which is spiritual as opposed to that which is carnal. We need to be serious about our service to God. We need to study the inspired Word of the one who is the foundation of our hope.

The world has nothing to offer us of any lasting value. The silver and gold will one day melt with all of the other elements in this world (II Peter 3:10-12). The pleasures of this life will pass away and, in fact, are even now passing away (I John 2:17). We must not go back and conform ourselves to the lusts of this world. Instead, we must be holy. God is holy. In His eternal abode of heaven there is nothing that defiles. We must want heaven more than we want anything or anyone here on this earth. To be with God in eternity, we must set ourselves apart for His service in humble obedience while we are here.

Our hope is real because it is firmly founded in God. What a glorious fulfillment of our hope will be realized when we see our Lord and hear Him say, "Come, you blessed of My Father, inherit the kingdom prepared for you from the foundation of the world." (Matthew 25:34).

The Day is coming. What a day it will be for the faithful Christian when the Lord comes again. Our hope will find its fulfillment in our eternal victory. "He who testifies to these things says, 'Surely I am coming quickly.' Amen. Even so, come, Lord Jesus! The grace of our Lord Jesus Christ *be* with you all. Amen." (Revelation 22:20-21).

EXERCISE YOUR MIND

True or False

1. No human knows when the Day of Judgment will be. ☐ T ☐ F
2. The Day of Judgment will be a time of victory for the righteous and sorrow for the unrighteous. ☐ T ☐ F
3. The Day of Judgment will be a time of reunion for those who have been faithful to God. ☐ T ☐ F
4. Resurrection is a fact. ☐ T ☐ F
5. Death is going to be destroyed. ☐ T ☐ F

Multiple Choice

1. The second coming of Jesus:
   A) will come without any signs, as a thief in the night;
   B) will be proceeded by multiple signs;
   C) will initiate the thousand year reign of Jesus on earth.

2. The apostle Paul:
   A) never thought about heaven;
   B) often spoke of the hope of the resurrection and heaven;
   C) did not believe in the resurrection.

3. First Corinthians 15:
   A) teaches that there will not be a resurrection of the dead;
   B) questions the validity of the resurrection;
   C) provides abundant evidence for the truth of the resurrection.

4. If the resurrection is not a fact:
   A) Christians are to be pitied;
   B) it doesn't matter;
   C) we can be joyful.
5. The world offers us:
   A) all the reward we can ever have because heaven is not real;
   B) true peace and happiness;
   C) nothing of any lasting value.

Fill in the Blanks

(Note: All scripture quotations are taken from the New King James Version and can be found in this lesson.)

1. "But the _____ of the _____ will come as a thief in the _____, in which the _____ will pass away with a great _____, and the _____ will _____ with fervent _____; both the _____ and the _____ that are in it will be _____ up."
2. "Then we who are _____ and _____ shall be caught up _____ with them in the clouds to meet the _____ in the _____. And thus we shall _____ be with the Lord."
3. "I have _____ in _____, which they themselves also _____, that there will be a _____ of *the* _____, both of *the* _____ and *the* _____."
4. "For I _____ to you first of all that which I also _____: that _____ died for our sins according to the _____, and that He was _____, and that He _____ again the _____ day according to the Scriptures."
5. "So when this _____ has put on _____, and this _____ has put on _____, then shall be brought to pass the saying that is written: '_____ is swallowed up in

_____.' 'O Death, where *is* your _____? O _____, where *is* your victory?' The sting of death *is* _____, and the _____ of sin *is* the law. But thanks *be* to _____, who gives us the _____ through our Lord Jesus Christ."

Questions for Discussion

1. Why do you want to go to heaven? _____

2. Why will the Lord not give any signs of His coming? _____

3. What will be the standard of judgment used when the Lord comes to judge us? _____

4. Does knowing that with each passing moment we get that much closer to eternity make you sad or happy? Explain your answer. __

Hope's Ultimate Fulfillment   151

5. Why do some not believe in the resurrection of the dead? _____

6. What would life be like if Jesus had not risen from the dead?

7. How does knowing that death will be destroyed give us hope? ____

8. Discuss the blessings of heaven that are noted in Revelation 21:4.

9. What blessing or blessings of heaven are you looking forward to the most? _____

10. Why does God want our hearts focused on heaven rather than on things of this world? _____

11. What can we do to keep our focus on heaven?

12. What does it mean to be holy?

13. Is there anything in this world that is worth having if it means losing your soul to have it? Explain your answer.

14. Do you know anyone who needs the hope of heaven? If so, what can and will you do to help them find it?

15. Can you overcome the world and be faithful to God unto death? If so, how?

_____

_____

SEARCH THE SCRIPTURES

(Note: For this section, you will find a good concordance helpful. All scripture quotations are taken from the New King James Version.)

Where is the following Bible verse located? _____

"That having been justified by His grace we should become heirs according to the hope of eternal life."

Appendix

God's Plan of Salvation

The Bible teaches that you and I are sinners (Romans 3:10,23). As such, we are displeasing to God (Psalm 5:5). Our sins, like a brick wall, separate us from Jehovah (Isaiah 59:1,2). They separate us from the one who is going to judge this world, the one who has the power to cast us into eternal hell or take us into eternal glory in heaven at Judgment (Matthew 7:21-23; 25:31-46).

Certainly all of us want to avoid the punishment of hell and go to heaven, but how can we accomplish this desire if we are sinners who stand separated from God? Were it not for the grace of God, we could not accomplish it at all (Matthew 19:25,26; Titus 2:11).

Ephesians 2:8 states, "For by grace you have been saved through faith, and that not of yourselves; *it is* the gift of God." That "the gift of God *is* eternal life in Christ Jesus our Lord." (Romans 6:23). Prompted by His perfect love, God gave His only begotten Son, Jesus the Christ, as a sacrifice for our sins (John 3:16). The penalty for sin has to be paid. Because of God's grace and love, He does not want us to have to pay that penalty (though we hasten to mention that God's perfect justice demands punishment for those who do not obey the Lord – Deuteronomy 32:4; II Thessalonians 1:7-9). The blood of His Son that was shed on a cross on the hill of Calvary nearly 2000 years ago paid the price for sin.

Our sins CAN be forgiven. We CAN be pure in the sight of God IF we will be washed in the soul-saving blood of Christ that is made available to every sinner. But how are we washed in this blood? God's grace saves us, but His grace alone does not save. It is by His grace that everyone has the opportunity to be saved and it is by His grace that some will be saved, but not everyone will be saved in eternity (Matthew 7:13,14). Only those who obey the Lord's Gospel and thus are washed in the blood of Christ have the hope of eternal life (Revelation 1:5).

Again referring to Ephesians 2:8, we learn that faith plays a part in our salvation. By His grace, God provides salvation but WE must do something to receive it. We must believe (have faith) not only in Him (Hebrews 11:6), but also in Jesus as the Christ, the Son of God (John 8:24). BUT, faith alone is not sufficient to save us from our sins (James 2:24). James 2:19 says that the devils believe, but they are not saved. Faith that is not put into action is a dead faith that is useless (James 2:20).

The New Testament very clearly tells us how to act on our faith so as to secure the blessing of forgiveness of sins. With the faith that we gained from God's Word, the Bible, firmly planted in our hearts and minds (Romans 10:17), we learn from the Bible that we have sinned against God. Knowing that we don't want to continue our lives as lost sinners, the next logical step for us to take is repentance. To repent means to change one's direction, to turn from one's devotion to Satan and turn to a devotion to God. Jesus stated that we all MUST repent (Luke 13:3). Peter indicated the same in Acts 2:38 and 3:19.

Faith and repentance are still not enough to secure Divine forgiveness. In the New Testament book of Acts, sometimes called the book of conversions, we have an example of a believing, penitent sinner making a public confession of Christ. "I believe that Jesus Christ is the Son of God," he declared. (Acts 8:37). Jesus had earlier stated that confession of belief in Him was necessary (Matthew 10:32,33). The apostle Paul later wrote that confession is made unto (in order to receive) salvation, "For the Scripture says, 'Whoever believes on Him will not be put to shame.'" (Romans 10:10,11).

Faith, repentance and confession still fall short of the soul-cleansing power of the blood of Christ. II Timothy 2:10 says that salvation is IN

Christ Jesus. The alien sinner has to get INTO Christ somehow, but nowhere does the Bible say that we can believe into Christ. Nowhere does Sacred Scripture tell us that we can repent into Christ. The Divine record contains not one statement that says we can confess into Christ. How then can we get into Christ and have our sins washed away by the blood of the Lamb of God (Hebrews 9:13,14)?

One passage of the Bible answers this question for us. Galatians 3:27 speaks of people who had been baptized (immersed) INTO Christ. Verse 28 speaks of them being IN Christ Jesus. They got there by virtue of their immersion into Christ.

The absolute necessity of immersion to be saved is taught in several New Testament passages (Mark 16:16; Acts 2:38; Acts 22:16; Romans 6:3ff; I Peter 3:21). This immersion is to be the one authorized by the Father, the Son and the Holy Spirit in God's Word (Matthew 28:19). It is the one immersion mentioned in Ephesians 4:5, namely, immersion in water for the forgiveness of sins through the blood of Christ.

Faith, repentance, confession and immersion for the remission of sins are God's commands that we must obey if we want to be saved. These are not man-made works, for no one shall be saved by works that man creates (Ephesians 2:9). These are acts of obedience that God has mandated in His Word, acts that we MUST do if we want to break down the wall of sin that stands between us and Him.

Following these steps of salvation and rising up from the waters of immersion, a person becomes not only a new creature (II Corinthians 5:17), but he or she is then a member of the Lord's church, the one and ONLY one Jesus promised to build (Matthew 16:18). The Lord adds the saved to the church (Acts 2:47).

His church is not a denomination but is the one body into which all who want to be saved in eternity must come (Ephesians 1:22,23; 4:4-6; 5:23). Only those who have obeyed the Gospel and thus become members of the Lord's church can scripturally be called Christians (Acts 11:26).

Won't you, dear reader, look at the scriptures that have been cited, examine them carefully and let them sink deeply into your heart? Won't you then muster the courage to obey the Lord? Your sins will be washed away, you will become a servant of the Lord (Romans 6:17,18) and a part of His family (Ephesians 3:10-15) and you will have the hope of eternal life (Titus 1:1,2; I John 2:25), a hope that will become reality in Judgment if you will only continue to follow the Word of God all the days of your Christian life on earth (II Timothy 4:7,8; Hebrews 10:36). May God bless you as you do His will.